# NO TIME TO BE DUMB

# No Time to Be Dumb

LETTERS TO TEENAGE GIRLS

Rachel Jankovic

CANON PRESS

MOSCOW, IDAHO

Rachel Jankovic, *No Time to Be Dumb: Letters to Teenage Girls*


Published by Canon Press
P. O. Box 8729, Moscow, Idaho 83843
800-488-2034 | www.canonpress.com

Cover design by James Engerbretson
Interior design by Belle Iverson
Illustrations by Josiah Nance
Printed in the United States of America



ISBN: 978-1-59128-324-9



*Library of Congress Cataloging-in-Publication data is on file with the publisher.*

25 26 27 28 29 30 31 32 33 34 10 9 8 7 6 5 4 3 2 1

# Contents

## Recipes & Lists

*To my lovely daughters,*

*with so much love and admiration.*

# Preface

Years ago I spoke at a conference in a room that turned out to be too small for how many women attended. The title of my talk was *Loving the Little Years: Motherhood in the Trenches* (the title of my first book), which should give you some idea of the makeup of the audience.

It is hard to describe the power in that room, but it remains one of the most visceral experiences I have ever had. Every seat was filled, and women were standing in the back and sitting on the floor right around the podium. But what made it feel so otherworldly was that almost every woman was pregnant or holding a nursing infant or sitting with a toddler in her lap. The depth of life and the unbelievable power of it all was overwhelming.

> Who is she that looketh forth as the morning, Fair as the moon, clear as the sun, And terrible as an army with banners? (Song of Sol. 6:10, KJV)

It was that glorious passage that came to my mind—because in that moment I could see, truly *see* something about these women that is not usually so visible. They were terrifying and they didn't even know it.

I have a similar feeling when I turn to speak to you young women. There is a force and a power here that is only just coming into itself. The potential is astonishing. Yet young women are very rarely aware of it. They very rarely feel urgent to steward it, very rarely see the import that their current behavior can and will have on hundreds, thousands of others. Your spiritual life is always a key point in a battle, and this is no time to be dumb.

The topics of these letters are mostly trivial in nature, but the intent behind them is anything but. It is in just these ordinary fields that young women can learn what it looks like to be a practical Christian woman who lets her faith shape her life rather than the other way around. This isn't meant to be an encyclopedic answer to all your questions or a theological treatise—the goal is to talk about some common struggles that might be too ordinary to be noticed or too awkward to bring up. Yet when they are addressed with the clear intention of living out your faith, they become powerful to shape.

It is my prayer that you young women will be shaped into weapons that the Lord will use mightily.

R.J.

# Note

While the girls in these letters are fictional, I really do have four teenage daughters, and they all have friends. "Lizzie" is my family nickname, and I use it here as a show of affection—this is what I might talk about with girls I love who are turning into women I admire, and I am glad to include you in that number.

LETTER 1

# Let's Begin

Dear Lottie,

Getting this request from you was a delight, and I am glad your mom suggested it! I would be more than happy to try to answer any questions that you and your friends have come up with. With four teenage daughters of my own right now, it will all be very relevant and present subject matter. In many ways it seems like only last week that your mom and I were doing our own growing up together as college roommates, straight through many of the same issues I see my own girls and their friends dealing with. I imagine you all will ask about a lot of the same things. So much has changed in the world, but when it comes to the work of becoming a mature Christian woman, so much is and will always be exactly the same.

I understand what you mean about this group of girls being very diverse, and no—I won't be shocked or bothered by any of the questions you ladies send me. I would especially welcome any follow-up questions (or outrage—be honest!). I might not be the youth of today anymore, but I am not deaf or blind to the kinds of temptations the world is offering now, and it is a blessing to me to give some outside guidance if I can. What a gift to have these friends in your life, interested in pursuing Christ together! I'll be praying that the Lord richly blesses your gatherings to discuss these things—I am proud of you for giving this a try, because it sounds like it will be a little stretch for you as the coordinator and hostess. I have no doubt the Lord will bless this effort of leadership and all the friendship dynamics that such a thing may expose—and I will be praying that He will use it greatly in all directions.

As for how to organize the questions, I don't think you need to. Just ask everyone what's bothering them most, and let's start with that. It doesn't really matter what the subject is—any real answer will always come back to Christ.

The chocolate chip cookies you wanted the recipe for—this makes a ton (fifty or so). You could always freeze half of the dough balls to use another week, although I bet with all those brothers of yours they will all get eaten!

Looking forward to round one!
Aunt Lizzie

# Chocolate Chip Cookies

YIELD: 50

## INGREDIENTS

- 2 c. (1 lb.) Butter (room temp)
- 2 c. Brown Sugar
- 2 c. White Sugar
- 4 Eggs
- 2 tsp. Vanilla
- 1 tsp. Salt
- 2 tsp. Baking Soda
- 2 tsp. Baking Powder
- 4 c. Oat Flour (just grind oats in a food processor)
- 5 c. All-Purpose Flour
- 1/2 bag Milk Chocolate Chips (my kids love Guittard because they are big)
- 1 bag Semisweet chocolate chips

## DIRECTIONS

1. Preheat your oven to 375 degrees. Start by creaming the butter and sugars in the mixer (a handheld mixer works fine, too) until the blend is light and fluffy.
2. Add eggs one at a time, beating well between each egg before you add the next. Everything ought to be very fluffy and light at the end of the eggs!
3. Add the vanilla, then stop the mixer while you combine the dry ingredients in a separate bowl. Add them to the batter and mix on low until they're just incorporated with no dry spots. Then add the chocolate chips and mix briefly.
4. Put golf-ball sized dough balls on parchment-lined baking sheets (I use a scooper to quickly shape them all).
5. Bake at 375 degrees for 11–12 minutes. The cookies should be barely (barely!) starting to get golden on the edges when you pull them out. I pull the parchment sheet off the pan onto the counter to quickly cool the cookies down so you can handle them. Enjoy!

LETTER 2

# Modesty

Dear girls,

I told my husband that I bet the first round of questions would be about modesty, and you ladies did not disappoint! Modesty is always a fresh and burning topic and probably always will be. We live in a world where fashion is changing constantly, and with each new popular look there is usually a different kind of immodesty opportunity that goes along with it. I have lived through Christian women heatedly arguing over whether you can show your stomach below the belly button with short shirts and low-rise pants, whether you can wear yoga pants as pants about town, whether shirts with cutouts here and there are appropriate, whether backless dresses are too suggestive, whether you can wear straight up leggings with no underwear, etc. I imagine this will be the case forever—because whatever culture you are living in, it is there that you need to learn and practice modesty.

I love the honesty of your questions, especially because it clearly shows your frustration with the sorts of things you've been told about why you must be modest and about what modesty really means anyways. There has already been a great deal of conversation and arguing on modesty, which means there are thousands of ways to be aggravated, annoyed, and sick of everyone whenever this topic is on the table. The frustration is ready made, as it were. And yet—the very fact that we are all tempted to be mad about the conversation itself reveals that the subject really does cut close to the heart. It was and has always been relevant.

Whenever modesty comes up, strange things start happening. Older women, anxious to persuade the younger women, start spewing forth reason after reason for The Modesty, many of which seem antiquated or silly. Younger eyes roll, which acts as fuel on the fire. The older women become more and more earnest, pleading with you to take them seriously. The trouble is that the more earnest they get, the easier they are to mock (even just in your head). You are thinking that if their outfits are what modesty is, you'd rather take a pass. Perhaps their examples so clearly call up an antiquated aesthetic that it seems entirely irrelevant to you.

My theory is that these earnest arguments from the church ladies are often just mislabeled testimonials. Most mature Christian women have some moment or some thought that slapped them in the face back in the day and caused them to understand it all, finally. Things like "If you don't want your future husband to see that much of her body, you ought not to show that much of yours." Or "When I got married and realized how much of a struggle lust is for men, I no longer wanted to wear my tight little skirts." They keep getting it out of their scrapbook of concepts, thinking it's an irrefutable truth that you will not be able to resist. The more you resist, the harder it comes at you. More pleading, more somber warnings.

But this is an opportunity for you to simply have charity. When someone wants to tell you how God taught her something, just let her. You will be surprised at how, later, when the Lord has grown you up over time, you will find yourself much more sympathetic to those stories. You will quite possibly have one of your own to contribute to the discussion. My point is simply that the stories the church ladies are telling you are not actually the main reason you have to be modest—they are probably just testimonies to the first time that they realized how *good* modesty actually is.

As a college student I once witnessed a fat and deeply unattractive man sitting like a slackening wad of dough on a bench in dirty sweatpants. He was inexplicably wearing a clear fluorescent yellow visor, which cast an eerie pallor over his already troubled complexion but did nothing to hide his thinning hair. I watched him stare, open-mouthed, at the legging-clad buns of a young woman who was walking by holding the hand of her boyfriend. It was a strange and shocking moment of revelation for me—the moment when I realized what lust actually looks like and why I didn't want to be turning heads in that way.

But I can see, as I imagine you do, that this very persuasive moment in my life is not a clear biblical argument. I tell you all of this so you can see that I (1) am a true church lady myself, and (2) am warmly inviting you all to join me.

Keep in mind that the older women in your life grew up in eras when different things were cool. I don't mean different cuts of pants, but different character traits. The oldest among us grew up in an era when it was broadly *cool* to be lovely, lady-like, mannerly, and polite. Then there are those who grew up in the "cool to be free-spirit hippies" era, or the rebellious and ironic era. It is natural but not necessarily effective for women from another era to pull from what they believed and may still believe is cool while trying to persuade you. This is why it is so easy for you all to be dismissive of them. Perhaps even more provoking is the younger woman who rushes around like an old prude telling girls that they "must guard the hearts and eyes of the young men"—as though the lust of the boys was a burden laid by God directly on the shoulders of the nubile young women.

There are so many things to say on this topic, but I would like to keep it painfully simple. All of the reasons that modesty is a good idea, and all of the reasons that modesty is inconvenient for you, can be swept together into a big pile and saved for later. Actually, they can just go home—if you need them, you can give them a call. The reality is that modesty is simply a requirement for Christian women. If you are a Christian and you are a woman, modesty is not optional. Once you have come to terms with that very simple truth, the whole discussion can be edifying and encouraging. But until you have submitted yourself to God's Word on this matter, almost everything about the discussion will provoke or anger you. It's simple, if not easy. Do you profess Christ? Then you must be modest. Do the work to accept this before God and God alone, and you will suddenly have a much easier time talking about it with all the other ladies.

You're no doubt familiar with this verse from 1 Timothy:

> I desire therefore that the men pray everywhere, lifting up holy hands, without wrath and doubting; in like manner also, that the women adorn themselves in modest apparel, with propriety and moderation, not with braided hair or gold or pearls or costly clothing, but, which is proper for women professing godliness, with good works. (1 Tim. 2:8–10)

Something that we often gloss right over here is the fact that Paul says "in like manner." What manner is that? "Without wrath and doubting." I think you could generally describe the entire discussion surrounding modesty as a great cacophony of wrath and doubting. Yet here we are told to adorn ourselves in a manner without wrath, without doubting, with propriety and moderation, not outrageously, not ostentatiously, and with good works.

I'm sure that through the weeks I will keep coming back to this particular concept, because it is incredibly important for every one of you right now. As you are coming of age, you are exiting one phase of life and entering another. You have all been in a church where there are some community guidelines, constraints that have simply been imposed on you. You have been bowling with bumpers in the gutters. You know how to walk the line of wearing something that might make your mother a little uncomfortable, or might agitate a few church ladies, while pretending that you really have no idea what is happening. But now you have reached a threshold in your lives where the virtues of others will no longer be enough. No dress code exists beyond a certain age. Your mother's convictions cannot carry you from here on out. In all areas of your life, it is time for you to take hold of what you believe and make it your own.

So start by acknowledging that being modest is a requirement of—YOUR OWN faith, not a function of the only pants your mother would buy you, or what is allowed at school. You are all reaching the moment where what you wear and how you dress is a statement of what you believe to be true, good, and beautiful. Having acknowledged that fact, I want you all to look at your own closets and your own hearts honestly and make a decision FOR YOURSELF about something. Are those the shorts you tug down in the kitchen at home where Mom might see you and then pull back up when you're out of the house? Perfect. Start there. Get rid of them. I would say put some skin in the game of your faith, but I think a more appropriate image would be putting your skin inside some longer shorts.

Maybe there is a tee that you know to be a little tight, or a dress that swings up a little freely when you turn just so (as you may have practiced in the mirror), or a shirt that only meets up with your pants occasionally in passing, or a dress that shows a little cleavage when you bend over.

This is how the good work happens. It doesn't happen when you fight with the older women about what is modest and what isn't, or when you fight with your mother about the dress you really want to wear. It happens when you fight with *your own heart* about your lust to be lusted after. Look at it plainly. Take it and let it sit out in the open like a fat man on a bench in a fluorescent glow—and then repent of it. Turn away from it.

Now the whole reason we are having this discussion is that you want to mature—and being honest with yourself is vital to maturity. So I am willing to be honest with you too. I am not being mean to you, although I have no doubt that some of you have never endured such plain speaking. If it were in vogue to get out your smelling salts or fall into a swoon, you might be doing it. Where is a fainting couch when you need it? Yet it is in the plainness of my words that I hope to bless you. Stop pretending with yourself. Stop making those excuses about it all. Just look at it head on and acknowledge that not only does the biblical command for modesty apply to you, but it probably requires action from you to apply it faithfully to yourself for yourself.

Before we wrap up today's discussion points, I'd like to head a few things off at the pass, and just make a few claims. Feel free to kick back and let me know what I haven't persuaded you of.

"Modest" does not mean "ugly" or "boring"—you can and should want to look beautiful. But "beautiful" is not the same thing as "sexually available."

Prioritizing modesty does not mean that you assume the guilt of any man's lust problems—it simply means that you accept the responsibility of your own.

Modesty does, in fact, begin in the heart—but it also manifests on the outside (where it is commanded to manifest). Anyone who tries to keep modesty on the inside *only* is probably committed to keeping something else on the outside (maybe those leggings or your brand-new wedgie shorts). Take off the self-delusion about what is really going on in your heart and put on modesty in its place.

Without wrath, without doubting, adorn yourselves in modest apparel and good works. That's the mission, ladies! I'll be praying for you all—that God will give you clarity about what is happening in your own hearts and that He will give you real courage and a desire to make these virtues your own.

Many blessings,
Aunt Lizzie

LETTER 3

# Church Ladies

Dear girls,

I will start with your question about what to do with the "self-righteous" church ladies who are so clearly provoking to you. First, I want to acknowledge that I don't think you are imagining things—church ladies can be really annoying. They say it takes a village to raise a child, but it really only takes a few officious busybodies to alienate a whole generation from the church. And while you didn't exactly say it in your question, I can read between the lines enough to imagine that acknowledging yourself to be wrong in any way (even by deciding on your own to never wear that skirt or that T-shirt or that swimsuit again) may feel like giving a victory to *them*. The heart revolts!

But the long and the short of it is this: Jesus is either your Lord, or He isn't. What the other ladies are saying or doing or thinking has little or nothing to do with it. My grandpa used to say, "Never let a hypocrite come between you and God. That just means he is closer to Him than you are." So if you are continuing in disobedience just because you don't want to do what *they* think you should do, it's time to recognize that you are really leaning on them as a crutch to keep you from having to obey. It's not their opinions you don't want to accept but God's. Their annoying behavior is becoming your most precious possession—you actually want them to keep it going, because then you can keep the discussion about *them* and not about why you are still wearing something that you know dishonors the Lord. Any time you fixate on the scandal of someone else's opinion, there is a good chance this is what is happening.

Over the years I have had many opportunities to hear assorted unvarnished and patronizing opinions on the church ladies. They have their standards, and they appear to do things the way they have been doing them forever. Born with practical purses at their sides and outdated haircuts. They are certainly unfamiliar with what is popular nowadays. It is easy to dismiss all of these women as not understanding you. How *could* they understand you when they appear to inhabit a different universe entirely? Church ladies—all those prudes! What do they even know? They aren't aware of your favorite influencers or what is actually cool these days, so how could they speak into your life—especially on any aesthetic questions?

But keep in mind that you are all currently at your peak—young and fresh and beautiful. Everything in your world that is "cool" also happens to be young. But these ranks of church ladies you want to look down on include a lot of women who were much "cooler" in their youth than you will ever be. It's just facts. They aren't women from a different world—they have been in your *own* world *longer than you.* They may not be communicating clearly or effectively or winsomely, but they almost certainly know more than you do.

Many, many Christian women came by their perspectives (the ones that seem so staid and tedious to you) the hard way. Walk into any church, and you are looking at women who have been forgiven much, saved from much. There are women who had abortions in their youth, who were raped, molested, or abused. There are women whose histories with drugs and boys and alcohol and attempted suicides would shock you—the very women who you are telling each other are a little *unaware* of what the world is really like. Even if they haven't been through anything like this themselves, they have certainly witnessed far more of the destructive power of sin than any of you.

Basically, the church ladies probably aren't what you think they are. But more importantly to our purposes here, *you* probably aren't what you think you are either. You think those older ladies don't understand you, but the real difficulty is that they understand you better than you want to admit. That's what makes them so annoying. They're seeing something in you that you would rather they not look at. It is the sin in you that kicks back at their input. Your immunity to serious, life-destroying, soul-sucking sin is simply not as great as you may think it is.

While it may feel like these ladies are making a big to-do about hemlines and bra straps, I doubt that is the extent of their concern. These little markers indicate what highway you are spiritually driving on. We cannot see into each other's hearts. But Jesus says that we will know one another by our fruit. With that in mind, does heavy makeup, fake eyelashes, and contouring mean much? Yes and no. On the one hand, we're talking about nothing more than a darker or lighter colored makeup in specific areas on your face. Big whoop. Look how silly the prudish old ladies are about a simple cosmetic trend! But on the other hand, your makeup says an awful lot about your idea of beauty (and where you are getting it from). Your jewelry, clothing, posture, interests—all of these things are out on the surface, and no one is invading your private life by *seeing them*. Nor are they being invasive when they bring them up for discussion, since you already brought the subject up in public. You wear those clothes and that makeup in order to communicate something about yourself to anyone who's looking.

Now the reason this can be so aggravating is that you cannot present this sort of living artwork without people drawing their own conclusions from it immediately. They aren't waiting for you to explain it in words to them. The older women also know that they are not the target audience. They are not whispering to each other (or thinking to themselves) things like "She is soooo hot!" or "Wow! What a sculpted cheekbone!" Instead they are looking around wondering who this is for, wondering why you are holding yourself so cheap, wondering when you were discipled by a Kardashian in the ways of womanhood, and wondering who hasn't had the nerve to tell you the truth.

When the young church girls start adopting a porn star or drag queen aesthetic, taking photos of themselves with their cheeks sucked in and their lips pooched out, and talking about social media as though it's reality—that matters! It matters to the whole church because it indicates we have a bunch of Christian girls buzzing down a freeway without evaluating where they are going or why. And instead of talking about where they are going or why, the discussion keeps coming back to some version of "How dare those women notice! So judgy! As if they know anything at all about what I believe!" Picture it: a group of young women, hair flying in the breeze, screaming down the cultural freeway together, yelling to the older women, "What are you even talking about? We aren't *going* anywhere! This literally means *nothing*. You are so uptight! Loosen up!"

It will do you all a world of good to simply acknowledge that your makeup, clothing, hair, posture, and comportment are all communicating all the time. That's why you are doing it. No one just decides to have hair covering their face. No one just decides they need poochy poison lips and sunken-looking cheeks. Fake eyelashes and contouring are not time-saving convenience products—they mean something. Wearing torn clothing, or jeans that are specially designed to give you a wedgie—these are not things a person does for no reason at all. Forgoing underwear so that your pants or shorts can ride up tremendously and your buns can move freely is not something you do because it is comfortable. Also, it is manifestly not the kind of thing that happens accidentally—it is an effortful decision. So if people comment on your decision, you have to realize that you are the one who brought it into the public discourse.

Now it IS perfectly possible to be doing these things without having noticed the reason—to have drifted along being influenced culturally without asking yourself what it means and why you are doing it. But the big lie that young girls (and many grown women!) want to tell themselves is that there is no meaning or trajectory to style choices at all. It really isn't something that matters one way or another. The secret to maturity here is going to be taking responsibility for the decisions you are making about how you adorn yourself.

What is this look saying? Is it true? What does your favorite style say about women, about God, about sex? It can help to work through the idea from the other direction until you have practiced thinking this way. If you were going to make up a character who hated being a woman and had a bad relationship with her dad, what would she be wearing? What about a sexually available "mean girl"? What about a girl who is dabbling in witchiness and earth worship? What about a girl who is confident, virtuous, and respectful toward her parents? We are all actually fluent in this language. No one who is in a healthy relationship gets a bull nose ring and wears shirts with obscenities on it. No one. Tattoos, partially shaved haircuts, crazy dye, long and tangled hair, heavy makeup, extra-long fake nails—they all *mean* things, and we know it.

One of the funniest things about this whole discussion is that Christians seem to be the only people committed to acting naive about it. That's because Christians are the only people trying to indulge in these things *as hypocrites*. Girls with no religious affiliation have no reason to pretend that what they are wearing does not say "total despair" to everyone who sees it. They have no reason to pretend that their clothing choices aren't screaming "hooker without pay." That's *the point*. When a woman with a shaved head poses to show off her hairy armpits, what is she saying if not "I despise the cultural expectations of femininity and challenge you to do so also"?

Here's a fun activity that you all should do together: each of you find a style or a look and just discuss what it is saying and how it is communicating that. Is this style saying things that you believe are true? Why? Why not?

What you should want your clothing to say about you is that you are a woman who fears the Lord. It should say that you are clothed in strength and dignity. It should say that you are pure and faithful, that you will make a wonderful wife and mother. Do you look like you have hope? Like you know forgiveness? Like you are not beguiled by sin, or self-indulgent? Here's the thing—what you wear does not need to have a statement of faith printed on it, but it needs to be *entirely consistent with your faith.*

I'm going to have to leave it there for today because I have hungry children coming home soon who will be expecting dinner, but blessings on all of you!

With love,
Aunt Lizzie

LETTER 4

# Bad Influences

Dear Lottie,

I am glad to hear that your get-togethers are going well, even if it has felt a little awkward. So much of hospitality feels herky-jerky until it slowly becomes more natural. It's hard to tell if you get better at it or if you get more accustomed to the awkward. Either way, it is well worth doing, and I'm glad the cookies turned out!

About the girls who aren't participating in the discussion—of course include them as you can, and give them opportunities to talk, but don't make being pouty the best way to become the center of attention. The fact that they are rolling their eyes and whispering to each other is fine—welcome, even! Don't take offense for yourself, and certainly not on my behalf. This is a great chance for you to be a leader, and it is important that you not be easy to ruffle or fluster. Just stand your ground, be friendly, and don't be afraid of them. Don't let their attitude pressure you in any direction.

Putting the pieces together with what you asked and what your mom mentioned to me on the phone, I'm thinking that these two girls in part inspired these get-togethers? A couple of girls that you grew up with who seem to have taken a hard turn in the last year? Immodest, flirtatious, suddenly worldly, a little shameless?

I will try to help in my next letter to the group, but I wanted to mention something practical for you to keep in mind. (Obviously I don't really know the context—I've never met the girls, I can't see the way they look or act, etc. So you'll have to take this as a general principle rather than a particular conclusion.)

In my experience, "shameless" behavior is usually the opposite—meaning that it is usually driven in large part by very active *shame*. It may be shame over someone else's sin (parents' divorce or sin, unhappy home, feeling rejected by parents, having been molested in the past), or it may be shame over their own sin (porn use or other sexual sin, self-loathing, cutting, an eating disorder, alcohol or drug use, etc.). Oftentimes the first category inspires the second (for example, self-loathing often follows feeling rejected).

I mention this to you for this reason—it is always very possible for Christians (particularly young ones!) to spend a lot of time warning each other not to fall into sin while making someone who is currently (but secretly) entangled in sin feel further and further OUT. That shame (feeling like the fallen woman among the good little girls) can quickly cycle out of control. Where can a girl like this go to fit in? Probably back into the groups she shouldn't have been hanging out with in the first place. It is possible for every lifeline you feel like you are throwing to be received like additional condemnation. When a proud heart is still in sin, the way it will receive what they believe is condemnation is almost always by accusing others. They have personal reasons for wanting everyone to turn out to be hypocritical and false. This is why it is very important for you to not let your own feelings get wound up. You need to be non-reactive and clearheaded.

I recommend you keep loving them, praying for them, and including them while maintaining your own standards. This means, obviously, being kind to them, but it excludes loving them by bending to whatever it feels like they want. Make a point to pray for opportunities to talk with them about what is really going on. Ask the Lord to give you insight. Make sure that the presence of forgiveness is felt. You don't want to be a group of girls whose whole focus is the good advice you have for each other—instead, make sure that the unbelievably better Good News is what you are talking about. This is harder in groups that have grown up professing Christ together. We spend a lot of time sharing good advice—ways to apply and work out your faith. But if someone is in doubt about the essential things (like "Is there forgiveness for someone like me?"), then all the good advice in the world will feel like an unbearable weight.

Don't be afraid to say something (terrifyingly blunt) like "You seem unhappy—why is that?" You shouldn't try to force someone to confide in you, but don't pretend to be ignorant of something obvious either.

Whenever I feel like I need to talk to someone about something heavier or more awkward, I ask the Lord to give me an opportunity and the courage to take it. That way, when, out of the blue, they ask you for a ride somewhere, you know that this is God giving you the go-ahead. Take your shot. They may not want to share with you, but prepare yourself—if they do, you may be shocked by what they have actually been going through or participating in. I will try to do a little groundwork where I can, but all we can really do is pray for them and trust the Holy Spirit to be working.

Another random piece of counsel: When someone confides in you about something that you don't know how to deal with—don't! Use the authorities that God has put in your lives: parents (hers or yours), pastors, elders. Feel free to promise discretion, but never promise secrecy. Be a lifeline out of her problem, not just another person for her to commiserate with and loop into her secret sin!

Many years ago now, I asked a woman (who was in leadership at a Christian ministry) if she was sleeping with her boyfriend after she had let far too many clues slip out. When she responded to me that she "struggled with that," I was horrified—but far worse to me was the fact that, in the aftermath of that conversation, I learned that she had a number of Christian women friends who were all aware of the sin and were content to let it be a struggle.

Especially when someone young in a Christian community falls into sin, this can be a problem. The sinner confides in friends who are as out of their depth as she is. No one knows the way out, so everyone ends up bogged down by it. Don't be a "prayer warrior" who's absolutely useless because you never take any biblical action. Recognize that you may be the answer to those prayers by having the courage to provide actual accountability. Maintain your confidence in Christ, in forgiveness, in the basics of confession of sin and repentance, and be brave enough to actually help!

Until next time,
Aunt Lizzie

LETTER 5

# Wasting Time

Dear girls,

At the center of the entire world and all of history is this: a whore made into a virgin bride. It's very important we understand that. The church is the whore, restored from great unfaithfulness. Individual Christian women have been through the same transformation.

I know that many of you, having grown up in the church, might be thinking somewhere in the back of your mind that there is always forgiveness, so why not live a little? Maybe you can get yourself an interesting testimony by being wild (just a bit) before you decide to settle down and marry and have kids and walk with the Lord. We might as well drink too much or dress like an unbeliever now because we can repent later. Some of the things I said about the church ladies in the last letter might even encourage this thinking. If a bunch of them were immoral in the past, why shouldn't you give it a try? You can always pull out of it later and no one will ever have to know.

But as it turns out, the apostle Paul addresses this exact line of thought in Romans 6:1–4:

> What shall we say then? Shall we continue in sin that grace may abound? Certainly not! How shall we who died to sin live any longer in it? Or do you not know that as many of us as were baptized into Christ Jesus were baptized into His death? Therefore we were buried with Him through baptism into death, that just as Christ was raised from the dead by the glory of the Father, even so we also should walk in newness of life.

Forgiveness does not remove the consequences of sin. Every sin can be forgiven—there is absolutely nothing that the blood of Christ cannot cleanse us from. But there are also sins that will have consequences for life. In Christian circles where the free grace of God is preached and believed, it is a temptation to dabble in sin and think that, because we confess it, it isn't leaving a mark on our life in any way. But forgiveness does not heal STDs. Forgiveness does not mean you won't need to tell your husband how you fell into sin with that boy from school. Forgiveness does not mean your parents have to pretend you weren't that foolish before.

Paul makes a simple point: as believers, we cannot live in sin. Instead we should walk in newness of life. For those of you who grew up in Christian homes, you can be very naive about what death is like. You want to flirt with sin a little. You romanticize it in your mind; you imagine yourself indulging in it (just enough to grow worldly-wise and alluring). But there is life, and there is death. All of the cultural momentum that surrounds us is flowing to death and dealing in death. You cannot autopilot your faith and expect to get holier and holier. You cannot assume that whatever you do and however you live will turn out okay because you are a good girl. Scripture makes it very clear that we need to be fully engaged (heart, soul, mind, and strength) in loving the Lord. We do not get to claim Christ in the Sunday morning part of our lives and then throw ourselves into a totally other kind of living for the rest of the week. This is true even if the other kind of living is only a life of the mind. I want to be very clear about this. If you are daydreaming in a way that does not become a follower of Christ, you are cultivating a garden of death in your heart.

If you are not walking with God and growing in Him and fighting your own sins on a daily basis, then you are not staying stagnant in one place—you are actively wandering somewhere else. You cannot pause your spiritual growth to come back to it when you get a chance and have it waiting for you as you left it, bright and cheery, on task and ready to go. In fact, the temptation to pause it, or come back to it, or focus on it later is actually a *part* of wandering.

People always say that time goes by so fast, but the actual truth is that there just isn't very much time. When you are young and inexperienced, you still feel like you have enough time in your life to do things that you care or plan to care very deeply about. But the reality is, you won't. It is worth prioritizing things now that you will always be glad you did. I don't just mean pursuing practical skills, although I would definitely encourage pursuing those. What I really mean is growing in godliness and wisdom. You can't afford the time that stupid sin will take. There is no time to have the dumb years. Quick repentance is very important, and forgiveness is always available to you. The longer you stretch things out ("I don't really want to stop flirting with this non-Christian guy at work, I don't really want to tell my parents that I snuck out, or lied, or watched a movie I should not have watched, or routinely look at porn on my phone"), the more of your life you are wasting.

Think of your spiritual life as a long walk down a hall. Bright, shining, beautiful light is streaming in through the windows. You know that you are supposed to go straight ahead and stay in the light. Even so, there are doorways off to the side. You know you aren't supposed to stray off course, but for one reason or another, the side rooms invite you all the same. Maybe you hear a lot of laughter in one, or you see a lot of cool people heading into another. Sometimes it's simply the lure of mysterious darkness. Maybe you just aren't looking where you're going because you're on your phone watching reels.

Whatever the reason for your desire to wander off, fight it and fight it with all you have. Because once you take a turn down a dark corridor, it can take a very long time to get back out of there. It doesn't matter how petty the sin is—it is big enough to fight.

My granddad was a man who loved preparedness. He would frequently confront us with random situational story problems to help us think through how we would handle ourselves. For example: "What would you do if someone jumped in your car with a gun and told you to drive them somewhere?" His answer? Get in a wreck as fast as possible so that you draw everyone's attention to the situation. One of the things that he was fond of telling us was to never, ever be moved from the first scene of the crime, because the second scene will always be worse. If someone is kidnapping you, have the showdown as soon as possible.

I realize that this may seem a little off topic—but imagine the hostage-taking gunman to be your own sin. That lust problem, that lie you really, really don't want to put right, that daydream about a married man that you think won't ever come to light or be noticed: it has a gun pointed at you and is telling you to drive to an abandoned warehouse. Have the fight—in all of its awkward glory—NOW. Do not delay. Do not hesitate to draw the attention of people who can help you. Do not let your sin make you drive off to a part of town where no one will hear you. Treat it like the enemy it is from the outset. Sin is always a kind of insanity. It is always a play to pretend that God is not actually in charge, that the one who made you is not in authority over you, that the world He created does not operate according to His design.

I guess the two things that I want you to take away from this are pretty simple. First, God saves sinners—and delights to save sinners. He forgives freely and generously, and that forgiveness is a glorious gift. None of us are saved because we behaved well, but rather because Christ and Christ alone is perfectly righteous.

And second, if you know Jesus, then you have no business living in any kind of darkness. It is not where you belong! Any time a Christian finds herself in a muddle—wandering around in some kind of spiritual gray area or darkness—there is only one answer. Cry out to God, repent, and get out of there!

The more seriously you take your own sin, the more mature you become. Fighting sin faithfully is the path of wisdom. More than just keeping you out of trouble right now, it makes you into a certain kind of woman—a faithful one, a virtuous one. Exercising those muscles of self-discipline will only ever be a blessing to you and to all of those in your life.

So here is what I want you all to think about and discuss with each other if you have time. What are some of the petty sins that really seem to sneak up on you? What are the first signs that you are stumbling into them? How are you letting your sin tell you where to drive? How can you deal with your sin more aggressively at that first scene of the crime so as to not have to visit the second?

Maybe you don't know how you end up storming off to your room again and again to slam the door after yelling at your mom. Well, what are the first signs of that sin? When it hops in the car with a gun pointed at you, what does it look like? How can you prepare yourself to put up a fight THEN and fight it out all the way to a victory? What would it look like if you did not simply surrender to and comply with that first impulse?

The point of this exercise is to give yourself mental practice getting the victory before the actual temptation arrives. This is an exercise that will serve you well your whole life through many different phases and kinds of temptations.

Many blessings!
Aunt Lizzie

LETTER 6

# Peer Pressure

Dear Lottie,

Glad you are going to keep on plugging along! Your mom filled me in on the wild time that happened last week. I'm sure it doesn't feel encouraging, but it really should be! When bad things are growing under the surface, it does no one any good to keep it all under there. It sounds like your conversation with those two girls was a great kind of awkward. Your mom said there were lots of tears and that there has been tons of emotional work going on since. I would absolutely view this as progress, even though everyone is shocked and upset. I'm really praying that the Lord will be working here; I know that we can trust that He is. What I love the most is how much of a gift this awkwardness is for you and the other girls. This is going to be a leadership challenge for you.

When childhood friends stop walking with the Lord, it is really easy for everyone to want to fight to keep everything the way it always has been. This can put tremendous pressure in the wrong places. I am proud of the way that you have been willing to just say the thing and stand by it—even when it makes you feel petty and ridiculous. It is not your faithfulness that's causing the controversy.

Making faithful people feel like they are being bizarrely and unreasonably uptight is a *tactic*. It is not an accident. If those two girls really thought that tiny shorts and crop tops say nothing in particular, they would not have made a big fancy point of wearing them to the church group where you were going to talk about modesty. They wanted to watch you other girls squirm. Your squirming IS the point. It is like they were simply daring you to acknowledge what you could see and daring you to be frank about it. They were right in that it did take courage! So keep it up, and don't worry about it. You are getting practice leading. Of course you might think of ways you could have handled it differently, but don't get mired in regret about it. You are learning from experience.

I understand why you wonder if confronting the issue was wise or if this is the sort of behavior that love should cover. While I do believe these two are hurting, their trajectory is very important. They know better, and have known better all along.

Do not treat them like they are coming from a completely lost and broken place. With someone who does not know the Lord, you will obviously need to overlook some presenting issues. The central thing that needs to be put right will change everything else; a new heart will make a new life. But a hardening heart should not be ignored. These two girls are sinning against a greater light. They want to pretend that modesty standards and morality standards are just some kind of a cultural thing. But they know better than that, and you do not need to take them seriously on this topic.

My guess is that if they have not gotten into sexual sin yet, they are certainly laying the groundwork for it. You mentioned that they hang out downtown with lots of makeup and what feels to you like a weird mood—that's just them making themselves available for moral stupidity.

The things that they said in the group are simply talking points of a sort of evangelical deconstruction. Whenever someone does a version of this deconstructing, they are usually just looking to justify sin. These two appear to be doing so in advance. They may not be sleeping with anyone yet, but only because no one has asked.

If they come again I would recommend a straightforward and painfully awkward approach. You do not need to argue about anything at all with them. They know they are wrong, and you know they are wrong. So if the conversation begins to head in that direction again—them talking about the abusive nature of purity culture or whatever—I would suggest you just interrupt. Say something like "We are not interested in arguing about this with you. Why don't we pray." And then pray, right there, that the Lord will have mercy on them, and that He will hedge them back from the soul-destroying foolishness they are dabbling in. Ask the Lord to show them the truth of their sin, and ask Him to use their lives for His kingdom.

If they stay after that (which would surprise me!), do not give them the floor again. There is a difference between refugees coming in FROM the world and apostles recruiting our number FOR the world. Do not be afraid to draw the line. Ask them to leave if they are going to be like that—just tell them that any time they want to behave like Christian girls, they are welcome back.

It is very important to not be shrill in this kind of conflict. What you want to preserve is an unbending kindness. I know your mom is going to be giving a heads-up to your pastor about what happened, and I mentioned to her that someone should check if there is an online counselor involved. With the prevalence of horrific therapy all over the internet, I have started to assume that whenever someone is acting out in a way that I would not have expected them to, there is a different voice in the situation that no one can see. The influence can be overwhelming and insidious. Just because an online counselor claims to be a Christian does not mean she will offer any Christian counsel at all.

Do not forget that there are other girls there. Your willingness to be awkward IS a kindness to the weaker girls, even if they are temporarily stressed out by it. Don't be angry, don't be agitated, but also don't budge! I'm so happy God is giving you such a good opportunity to grow up and do hard things. Well done!

I meant to send you a recipe for whoopie pies last time. Here it is now! I just make a simple cream cheese frosting to fill them. Depending on the season, I have made it differently (maybe adding a little peppermint extract or crushed candy canes to the filling for Christmas, or some green food coloring and Irish cream for St. Patrick's Day). Whatever you do, they are delicious, and the shape makes them look so homey and inviting. Using a cookie scoop helps keep them all the same size. I always bake them on parchment and just pull the whole sheet off to cool on the counter. A little dusting of powdered sugar on the finished cookies adds a nice contrast.

Many blessings,
Aunt Lizzie

# Whoopie Pies

YIELD: 24

## INGREDIENTS

- 1 c. Butter
- 2 c. Brown Sugar
- 2 Eggs
- 2 tsp. Vanilla
- 2 1/2 tsp. Salt
- 2 tsp. Baking Soda
- 4 c. Flour
- 1 c. Cocoa
- 2 c. Buttermilk

## FOR THE FILLING

- 16 oz Cream Cheese, at room temp
- 1/2 c. Butter, also at room temp
- 2 lb Powdered Sugar
- A splash of Vanilla

## DIRECTIONS

1 Preheat the oven to 350 degrees.

2 Cream together the butter and brown sugar.

3 Add the eggs in one at a time, and then the vanilla.

4 In a separate bowl, whisk together the flour, cocoa, baking soda, and salt.

5 Add the dry ingredients to the wet ingredients in batches, alternating with the buttermilk.

6 Scoop the dough into small balls and bake them until the tops spring back when touched—about 12 minutes.

## FOR THE FILLING

1 Cream together the cream cheese and butter until smooth, then mix in the powdered sugar and vanilla (or other flavoring).

When the cookies have cooled, take a cookie, spread some icing on the bottom of it, and sandwich it with another cookie. Dust with powdered sugar.

LETTER 7

# Emotions

Dear girls,

I'm glad to hear that the discussion last week was encouraging to you all! It sounds like a fruitful time from this distance because the questions you sent along were so good: they showed that you are really working through some things. I love that you all are thinking about what provokes you and why.

I'm going to lump a bunch of the questions all together. I think if we address emotions more broadly it will hopefully answer several questions at once. Emotions and emotional self-control will forever be a big topic for women. What we need to address at the outset is *what to do* when we feel a certain way. Maybe we feel sad or we feel angry or we feel hurt, and that creates an emotional environment where almost anything could set us off. Even if we acknowledge that all the things we said when we were angry were sinful, is it a sin to feel angry in the first place? Or hurt? Or just touchy? How do we fight big outbursts of sin at the outset, before things have escalated? And do we need to do so?

I want to take a quick minute to clarify something here. One of the questions mentioned PMS and other hormonal fluctuations, and that brings up something that is super important for all women to understand. When it comes to behaving like a Christian, there is no qualifier about where you are in your cycle. "Rejoice in the Lord always, again I say rejoice, unless you are crampy." "Be ye kind one to another, tenderhearted, patient, forgiving one another, unless you are PMSing, in which case by all means indulge, indulge, indulge yourself and perhaps have a chocolate."

The reality is that you will live your entire life in a physical body that has physical problems. God knows that. He knew that when He created you. So at no point do we need to go to the Lord to explain our physical temptations. And at no point do those physical temptations provide us with a legitimate excuse for our failure to obey Him. The Lord gave us His commands alongside the bodies we have. So you are more hormonal than you were last week, and that adds a little spice to the feelings you are having—that is to be expected. Your hormonal situation is not exactly unprecedented. You could literally write it out on the calendar: "This is a day when I am likely to be very sensitive, or feel like things are far worse than they are." Pray about it in advance and get used to expecting yourself to feel less reasonable at some times of the month. Just like you hopefully prepare for this situation in physical and practical ways, prepare yourself emotionally also.

So now that we're clear we do not get a big free pass to behave badly because we are emotional creatures with hormones, let's get on to the next layer on this.

I think it would do all women a world of good to stop thinking that our emotions are our really attractive feature. The temptation I face when my emotions are acting out is to start acting like my emotional trouble ("My work doesn't matter, I don't matter, no one cares, no one appreciates my work . . .") is the most important thing going on. But on any given day my calling is much bigger than my feelings. The reason it is important that I raise godly children is NOT so that I will feel appreciated (surprising!). The point of all the work I am called to do (and every Christian is called to do) is the glory of God—a thing that is infinitely beyond us.

As John Piper famously wrote, "God is most glorified in us when we are most satisfied in Him." Our emotions do have a purpose—but they REALLY are not the point. Your emotions are not the point of your friendships (you shouldn't make friends for the sole purpose of feeling accepted and loved). They are not the point of your schoolwork (you shouldn't do school for the sole purpose of feeling smart). They are not the point of any given situation. Making your emotions the point of your work has a horrible effect on everything you do: it turns it all upside down. Imagine trying to build an ice cream sundae—but you start with a cherry, then a cute little pile of whipped cream, then scoops of ice cream stacked up, all topped with a glass. There is a reason the most delicate things in our life don't belong at the foundation of everything we do. What makes a lovely flourish makes a terrible base layer.

Structuring your life on the foundation of how you feel makes you incredibly easy to sabotage. Our feelings are very easy to manipulate. Think of the difference in your mood when you wake up feeling like you lost a few pounds versus when you wake up feeling like you gained a few pounds. Or when the day is sunshiny and glorious versus when the day is unexpectedly cold and rainy. Or when a random stranger says something nice to you versus when a random stranger cusses you out for no good reason. These are all things that can impact the way you feel, but they have almost nothing at all to do with your actual duties. If things as trivial as these can affect us this much, it should be clear how easy it actually is to manipulate someone emotionally. All you need to do is direct one unkind remark to someone, and you can make them spend all day digging into how that made them feel. None of us should want to be this easy to deflect and distract and destroy. Don't allow your emotions to be recruited as foot soldiers on behalf of the Enemy.

If you treat your feelings like a god, they will start acting like one: a little petty monster deity. Many women cultivate their ugliest feelings as though they are hugely valuable and exquisite orchids, graceful, lovely, and rare. You can see this easily on social media, where women are quick to celebrate their ugliest emotional selves. "This is me, and I embrace my rage," or " I am just really loud and obnoxious and I expect everyone to deal with it." We act as though every passing feeling we have is something everyone ought to know and care about, even revere. I hope you have had the treat of seeing one of those clips of a nurse crying in a hospital hallway, with a caption like "When you lose a patient . . ." Of course, they had to set up their phone first and find the most flattering angle. The loss of perspective is almost incredible, but it has become almost expected in our time. True compassion in that instance would not think first of sharing her own feelings and sorrow.

When we make how we feel at any given moment the most important thing, it is like getting into a big inflatable sumo suit and taking ourselves super seriously: How dare our family and friends keep bumping into our enormous, artificially-inflated, emotionally-imbalanced, and hard-to-avoid selves! This kind of thundering around is not admirable, interesting, or beautiful. It is instead a way to make yourself the center of attention. You are becoming a big nasty puddle, increasingly hard to avoid, that no one wants to step in. Do not make the mistake of thinking that any attention is good attention.

You should practice listening for this behavior in yourself. For example, take a statement like this: "I feel like no one ever does anything thoughtful for me." Notice that this is a statement that no one can argue with. You FEEL it to be true. If you said, "No one ever does anything thoughtful for me," it would be different. People could point out thoughtful things that *have* been done for you. You could be fact-checked by others, and also by yourself. This is probably why we don't typically say things this way.

It is not a sin to have a feeling that does not accord with reality, but it IS sin to keep it there in your heart and mind and let it grow. It's a sin to tell lies to yourself, and then to listen to them and believe them. It makes no difference if the entire transaction is occurring in your head and heart. Your feelings are not the measuring stick. God's reality is. So when you have a big feeling, your immediate response needs to be to expose that feeling to TRUTH. Your mom does not ALWAYS say no to you. She does not hate you (take a moment to remember who picks you up from school every day and asks you how your day has gone). Having to start the dishwasher is not actually a form of slavery. Etc., etc.

To go back to those weeping nurse videos—an admirable woman in that situation recognizes that her grief over the loss of a patient is not the most important thing happening. She is there to serve people going through a far more profound grief. She is not the star of the show. Glorifying our wild emotional lives is actually a way of destroying the unique strength of women. We can be far more reliable, more generous, more kind, and more capable when we stop keeping one eye on how it is all feeling for us.

In some cases our feelings are really big because the situation is actually big—in those cases we need to hasten to refer to the Word of God, cling to it, and believe it in practice and not just in theory. Maybe you are going through a very real trial and you need to think about the reality that God knows what He is doing in your life. You need to think what it means to actually live like you believe those truths that you have always been taught.

But the super important thing is that there is a greater, real TRUTH outside of your feelings, and your feelings need to conform to that. This truth is anchored in God, in His Word, and in the objective reality that He made. This reality is the world that you want to be living in emotionally. It is possible to feel (deeply!) falsehoods. It is also possible to not feel (deeply!) truths.

Jesus says, "I am the way, the TRUTH, and the life" (John 14:6). We must constantly turn to Christ, the ultimate truth, to deal with our emotions. If you are diligent in looking to Christ to shape your feelings, you will become a much more stable woman. Stop looking within yourself and instead look outward and upward: to Christ. I don't mean imagining a picture of Jesus from a felt board in your childhood. I mean looking to His Word and obeying it. Remember the things that you know to be true and seek to conform your feelings to those glorious truths.

Living your life can be like climbing a cliff face. Little handholds and footholds along the way are all well and good when we are feeling capable and comfortable and strong. But those little encouragements are nothing when we face a real difficulty. Then the tender mercies of God are all found in the hard truths—the places where we are anchored so firmly to the face of this cliff. We are tied off safely by the character of the Lord Himself.

Maybe you don't know why God let something happen—but you know that "all things work together for good to them that love God, to them who are called according to His purpose" (Rom. 8:28, KJV). Maybe you are going through something that you didn't want to go through—but you know that "we are His workmanship, created in Christ Jesus unto good works, which God hath before ordained that we should walk in them" (Eph. 2:10, KJV). Maybe you don't like your body, or your family, or your talents—but "who art thou that repliest against God? Shall the thing formed say to him that formed it, Why hast thou made me thus?" (Rom. 9:20, KJV). Maybe you're afraid of what might happen in some scary or difficult situation—but you know that we need not fear, "though the earth be removed, and though the mountains be carried into the midst of the sea" (Ps. 46:2).

These truths are the deep comforts of Scripture—the truths that anchor our emotions to the Godness of God. When trials or sorrows or difficulties blow us off of our little footholds and our plans, these truths keep us from slipping and falling to our death. Godly women cultivate their relationship to such fixed truths, and these truths moderate their emotional responses. This is a good mental image for what it means to trust God. You believe that the truths that some people find so unsavory and harsh are actually the tender mercies of a loving God to you. You are SAFE and SECURE and can be STEADY in the love of the Father.

When David writes in Psalm 144 about the blessing of God on His people, there is a very notable description in the latter half of verse 12: "Our daughters may be as pillars, sculptured in palace style."

I want you to think about this verse, because in a single metaphor David describes a whole lot of glorious goals and purposes for women. The role of women in the kingdom of God is *structural.* They're pillars, holding the whole thing up. Courage, toughness, stability, integrity, beauty—it's all there! This kind of woman is lovely ("sculptured in palace style"). She loves much and feels much. But she is also strong and stable, anchored in deep truth and the Godness of God. She is not self-indulgent or fearful or worried or fragile or emotionally imbalanced or unpredictable and unreliable. When God blesses a people, women aren't accessories, or kites that blow away in a storm. Being a Christian woman is a glorious calling—and a necessary one. The work requires a kind of strength that women are uniquely made for and capable of by God's grace.

Every woman has a long way to go to really be this—but it is what we should *want* to be. It is all too easy to get off the track, to take off in a weird direction and never fact-check ourselves. We learn by imitation very easily and almost without thought, which is why some of these more outrageous social media displays are actually very dangerous. What's more, a woman who is handling herself really admirably is often difficult to find, because—guess what? She probably doesn't share it all on social media. Women who are getting a lot done in their life are quietly holding things up by the grace of God. They aren't putting on kite shows with lots of streamers and inviting everyone to come watch them.

There are many bad habits (that you may need to break) involved in emotional outbursts. If you freak out, you get attention, and maybe people will want to listen to your perspective. Maybe you will get assurances of love and affection. This cycle can be addicting—and because you aren't sure how else to operate, it can feel very scary to try to stop. But if emotional outbursts are a tool you use in order to feel valued or loved or important, you are in the process of becoming an unsteady woman. No man should want to be married to an unsteady woman, and no one wants to be raised by an unsteady woman. Many people are interested in following an unsteady woman on the internet in the same way that many people want to watch Captain Zit Popper on the internet, or go out of their way to look at the damage from a house fire.

At the end of the day, your emotions are only of any use to you or others when they are *truthful.* They can (and should) be taught to be truth-tellers. This is a natural result of faithful and intentional work, and the kindness of God.

You all are of an age where emotional discipline is one of the most important skills you can learn. It makes sense that this is a major area of temptation for teens. The world, the flesh, and the Devil are all interested in keeping you from developing these strengths. A Christian woman who has learned to hold her emotions accountable to the truth is a powerful force. She is a pillar in God's glorious and beautiful kingdom work—absolutely strong enough to build on. She is trustworthy and reliable, and her presence lends a lot of strength to those around her. Recognize the fact that your emotional steadiness is a spiritually strategic point. You can and should learn to control yourself and thus bless your descendants far into the future. On the other hand, you can and should *not* indulge yourself and lay a wobbly foundation for your future family. Which way do you want to go?

We have largely lost the generational perspective these days. Very few young women in your age range are preparing for (or even thinking about) being a grandmother. And yet that is where the exponential work of your life will take place. You are in a planting phase, and it will never do to forget that the harvest is coming. A faithful, stable mother and grandmother is a tremendous gift. It is something that you can be training to be now, and something that will yield blessing for decades to come. While it is never too late to begin, you are absolutely missing an opportunity if you waste these years.

If you feel like you don't notice anything about what is causing your emotional situations until you are in the middle of some kind of a big emotional event, these are a few things you can think about that might be helpful.

Look for the little lies. Look for the things that you are saying only to yourself in your own head. Look for the little narratives you tell yourself that spin a tale of woe about your circumstances. This internal storytelling is how we convince ourselves that we are correct, wronged, justified in our bad mood, left out, afflicted, belittled, unloved, uncared-for, etc. But often these stories are not fully true. It is very common to build up our own perspective by going over the things that have happened with a particular emphasis, or reading into other people's motives, or adding meaning to things. When my children leave dishes in the sink it is not the same thing as leaving me a note that says "I don't care about you." And yet I could (if I was in a sinful emotional state) act like this is what happened.

Be strict with yourself here. This kind of internal narrative is not a harmless pursuit. Making up partially true stories to justify your bad attitude is just another version of putting your thumb on the scales, which is a thing that the Lord hates (even if it is the scales of justice). Notice when you are recounting a grievance in your head and then going back to try new words or phrases. We do this kind of thing to find the perfect way to make people feel sorry for us, or guilty, or whatever emotional agenda we have at the moment. Instead of indulging this habit in order to justify your own bad behavior, spend time thinking of the other person involved as being more important than yourself. Be kind, not accusing.

Another major temptation, one that is new for your generation, is the untruthfulness of social media. You may be interacting with the virtual world with a total lack of reference to the truth. This is because there are a lot of ways to lie these days, and when it comes to social media, there are a lot of ways to vacantly consume and participate in those lies. I'm not even talking about the obvious great big lies (although you should certainly be aware of those). I'm talking about the ambiance of filters and edited photos and fake smiles and friendships that look better than all of yours do.

Do not cultivate a life of the mind that is full of FOMO, or envy, or anxiety about how you compare to others. On the other hand, don't present yourself through a wall of glamorous filters and fake positions either. You never want to start looking at your life through a lens of "what will post well," specifically to get other people to envy you. This is a life that is two-dimensional and false. It would be far better for you to opt out of social media entirely than to become accustomed to the lies it runs on. When using any kind of digital or social media, there is a temptation to want to post pictures that will make people feel sorry for you, or envy you, or admire you. But Christian women should not be professional emotional manipulators. This is an area of ourselves that we need to look very honestly and frankly at.

Another major thing you should work to notice is all of the times you use words (either in your conversation or just in your head) such as *always* or *never*. It is very typical for us to inflate the offenses against us with words like this. Try to notice it in yourself. We choose to use these words when recounting the offenses of others against us, but usually we would be shocked and hurt if others used them to describe our behavior. We want to judge others by their actions no matter their intentions, and ourselves by our intentions no matter our actions. This is just part of the human condition. Instead, we need to focus on the real truth.

Practice being *more generous* toward others than you think others need to be toward you. I hope that you want to be wise and kind and gracious. All of these characteristics are in opposition to accusations and assumptions. If you find yourself saying or thinking things like "She *never* includes me because she thinks she is better than me . . ." then you really need to get into the habit of stopping yourself with a word of truth. Christians are to be lovers of the truth. So hold yourself to that standard—and not just reluctantly because you have to. You should avoid stepping into little falsehoods more diligently than you avoid stepping in dog mess, and I do hope that you try to not do that!

I've got to go make dinner since the afternoon is advancing so quickly. If I have time I will pop back to write more before you all meet again, and you can just read both letters the same week. If not, I'll be back next week!

With much affection,
Aunt Lizzie

LETTER 8

# Handsiness

Dear girls,

Look at me finding another chance to write, and then going above and beyond and taking it! Emotions, as it turns out, are a big subject about which I find I have much to say.

I want to talk about your words to each other, which is another area where loving the truth plays a key role. Gracious words are a kindness—there are many times that you can bless someone by truthfully telling them something kind or encouraging, something you admire about them. But there are friendships where flattery is the basis of the entire relationship. If you were not telling lies to each other, you would not be friends at all. This is something that you all need to not develop a taste for. You must refuse to walk into it when it is offered.

By "walking into it" I mean responding in the expected manner, and going along with what is clearly required. Many years ago I had this experience at a pottery-painting party of all places. I am fairly artistic, but not an artist. Whatever I was working on failed to meet even my own standards—in other words, I was well aware that I was painting a pretty meh piece. Well, there was a woman there who started complimenting me, my artistry, my incredible eye for color, my abilities, and everything else you could think of. I could *feel* the expectation in the air between us: "What would you like to say back to me now? What do you think about *my* painting? Do you have a return compliment?"

It was painfully awkward because I was not playing along—I was shrugging off what she was saying, and I was not thanking her for her words because she obviously didn't mean them. And when she finally asked me directly what I thought of her work, I said something honest like "That is a nice green!" Probably because I was not playing along, she began soaring to greater and greater flattery heights. If I had just done what I was supposed to do and given her some flattery right back, then we could have been friends—back-scratching friends with no regard for the truth.

When you start training each other to need flattery, you start thinking that flattery *is* niceness. You start thinking that kindness *is* people falling all over themselves about your outfit or your haircut or how unbelievably talented you are. You start expecting a lot of petting and admiration. You can actually take a pretty secure girl with loving parents and a wonderful life and make her desperate to hear lies. This kind of thing is incredibly common on social media—social media can serve as a gateway drug to the habit of lying to each other. Observe the crying-faces and fire emojis and "I love you" and "omg how are you so gorgeous" and other completely inflated overblown and unrealistic comments. It is but the work of a few moments to plot out what happens next when a girl develops an urgent taste for this kind of feedback. She'll adjust both her audience and her content in order to get it. Have you ever wondered why so many girls who are not actually living on the streets are nonetheless essentially prostituting themselves on the internet as a hobby—for some cheap praise and attention?

I do not just mean in a sexual way (although that obviously happens too). There are metaphorical ways to prostitute yourself—to sell things that should not be for sale. For the sake of the dopamine produced by some likes or views, we are willing to share anything on the internet. Or give away the privacy of our children's life and home. Or invite the world to get ready with us in the morning. We have lost all perspective on the value of what is not for the public eye. We are so caught up in our need for flattery and attention that we are willing to give away anything to get it.

There are a lot of problems with developing a flattery sweet tooth, but one of them is that it leaves you vulnerable to dangerous men. Superficial flattering attention is the behavior of a man trying to get a woman into bed *in a dishonorable manner.*

That may have taken you by surprise, but this is really just one of the fundamental truths of the world—and one that you should certainly know about. When a man shows interest in a woman, he is either trying to get her into bed honorably (after making vows before God and witnesses to stay with her for the rest of his life), or he is trying to get her into bed dishonorably (for some short-term pleasure, with no worries about the consequences). Of course there are lesser versions of each of these intentions, but these are the only two paths.

If a guy comes up to you and tells you that you are unbelievably hot and that he just can't look away from you . . . what do you think that is? Does that sound like someone who is thinking seriously about his relationships and behaving righteously? Or does it sound like a man who is looking for some quick results? Cheap compliments, e.g., "You are super hot," are not the words of a godly man looking for a godly helpmeet. Nor are fire emojis.

If the Lord blesses each one of you with a godly spouse like we are absolutely praying He will, let me tell you something about that man. He will love and admire you in a *reasonable and rational* manner. He will not be blind to your faults and failings, he will not be falling at your feet due to your unbelievable beauty, and he will not wake up early to leave you notes about how he has never met anyone with even a fraction of your talent or looks or whatever. These are just facts. A godly real man will be looking for a godly real woman: a woman who loves the truth as much as he does. When he finds that woman, many things about her will delight him. But he will not be trying to lure her into a relationship with a trail of breadcrumbs—each one a flattering lie.

Now obviously, the relationship between friends and the relationship between spouses are pretty different. But there is a lot of common ground here because in a godly husband-wife relationship, friendship is a major component. Godly friendship is actually good and healthy preparation for marriage. (As a sidenote, when that man comes along for you, it will change your relationships with your girl friends, because he will be a friend, but also so much more.)

Back to the original point. You do not want, in any respect, to model your friendships after the way an ungodly man pursues a woman for his own pleasure. I am sure some of you are shocked that I would even bring such a thing up in the context of your exclusively female friendships—but if you can get past the ruffled feathers, I think you will see that I am right. Don't develop a taste for this kind of interaction. When a bunch of girls treat each other like this, they are not building each other up at all. Instead they are cultivating expectations that will leave them incredibly vulnerable. They are cheapening their friendships, discarding them for something both dangerous and worthless—all for the sake of some easy compliments and very fleeting feelings. Right now, your lies have relatively few immediate consequences. But by making a practice of lying to each other, you're setting yourselves up to be easy targets, gullible and vulnerable in situations where lies are much more dangerous.

When your closest and most trustworthy friends are routinely lying to you in order to play on your feelings, there really is no good outcome. Best-case scenario, you are developing a taste for foolishness in your life. This is horrible preparation for marriage, and no preparation at all for becoming a good wife and mother to an honest man. There is no world in which needing to be flattered is a strength.

While I am here, it makes sense to expand my offensive comments and say that you should be keeping your hands to yourselves as well. Snuggling with each other, touching each other's hair for no reason, holding hands, sitting on each other's laps, sitting between each other's legs, giving each other rubs, hugging each other when you have been apart for twelve minutes—none of these things are wise or acceptable. Even if this sort of behavior has become common enough to not surprise you, I'm here to say that it is profoundly not normal. You may actually become emotionally entangled in a way that *is* sexual (even if you have not yet noticed that). The friendships of young women with young women is an area in which the Devil loves to make hay. If you are struggling at all with feeling secure, it can be very tempting to take the cheap affirmation that appears to be so easily available to you. It feels like nothing is really at risk, since this is just your friend, and she is just another girl.

Just because everyone involved does not intend to be a lesbian—and just because you may be profoundly angry that

I'm saying this—does not mean you aren't behaving sexually with one another. (It's actually pretty simple to check. If you saw a girl and a guy behaving the way you and your friend are behaving, would you immediately see the sexuality of it? Or if your mother behaved this way with another woman, would you feel uncomfortable?)

Sometimes this sort of behavior grows in a group of friends simply because everyone is more comfortable enduring and adapting to the strange behavior than they are with an awkward confrontation. Someone starts petting your head, and it surprises you, but you can't think of a way to deal with it that does not seem rude. So you just sit there and let them continue.

But it is well worth the effort to keep your physical boundaries strong. One of the great pieces of wisdom for young women comes from the Song of Solomon, which is all about the right kind of sexuality: "I adjure you, O daughters of Jerusalem, that you not stir up or awaken love until it pleases" (Song of Sol. 8:4, ESV).

One of the ways that young girls should heed this advice is by simply not starting physical relationships with each other, and by stopping them promptly if they have already started. It is all too easy to develop a physical neediness that you shouldn't have until there is a godly man in your life and appropriate boundaries are surrounding the two of you. Do not stir up or awaken physical love until you can express it in a way that glorifies God. The physical relationship you will someday share with your husband is so important (in so many ways!), and there is no reason to add baggage or confusion to it in advance. Keep your hands to yourself.

Whatever awkwardness it takes to get and maintain appropriate boundaries is worth it. Once you stir up and awaken physical love, it is hard to control. You've created an appetite with no wise or lawful way to satisfy it. I think it would bless many teens to spend a moment reflecting on the fact that whatever you get into now is not going to be a secret forever. There will come a time when you need to tell your future husband how you handled your physical desire. You may need to discuss it in premarital counseling. The old proverb is very helpful (as silly as it may seem to use here): A stitch in time really does save nine. Confess and be done with sexual thoughts and temptations when they are little and haven't grown up into a beast you are trying to keep in the basement. Ultimately, there is no such thing as secret sin.

Since I am not in the room with you all as you read this, and since I haven't even met most of you in person, I have no way of guessing if this was awkward or embarrassing to read aloud together. I don't know if any of you are more physical with each other than you should be. In any case, I think this is important enough to say to you—and if it is awkward to hear, then it is even more important that I say it straight out. I am doing you the honor of treating you like near-adult Christian women who *want to know* if what you are doing is foolish.

At the beginning of this letter I talked about not getting on a diet of cheap lies and affirmations; I am bringing it home here with a suggestion of the kinds of truths that Christian women ought to be able to hear and receive. It's not flattering, no, and it might not even feel kind. But the truth really is freeing. It really is better to look at your own behavior honestly. So if this did sting, recognize it as the wounds of a friend which are, indeed, better than the kisses of a friend.

Until next time! If you are still speaking to me then!
Aunt Lizzie

LETTER 9

# Repentance

Dear Lottie,

I am relieved that none of the girls were being snuggly when you read this together! I'm glad that my letter did not end up putting any one person awkwardly on the spot. But I am also thankful that it seemed to poke a few eyeballs and create a little friction in the room. I am also really thankful to hear that I poked you right in the eyeball too, although I did not anticipate that!

Even though you may feel socially uncomfortable for a little bit, it is so much better to get these things out in the open where they can be discussed. Letting things drift in friend groups is easier by far than risking someone getting their feelings hurt—but that is the coward's way out, and ironically, it ends up making the problem infinitely more drawn out and painful. This is sort of what seems to have happened in this group. When someone starts the whole handsy approach to being friends, it is uncomfortable and awkward to resist it. Yet now you are having to deal with the fact that nobody did resist it for too long. It's not more fun to do it now, but it still has to be done!

It is *good* for you girls to get used to saying things to each other like "No thanks! That's weird." It is *good* for you to get used to calling sin "sin" with each other. It is *good* for you to be able to say, "You have ungodly movie standards, so no, I won't come watch another movie with you." If someone is complaining to you about her parents, it is abundantly healthy to tell her that she's in sin. You do not want to create a "safe space" inside your friendships where gossiping is "venting," and dishonoring your parents is "having a hard day." In the same way, just because someone says they are a more huggy personality type does not mean that everyone's standards for normal behavior need to change.

Since you have been put in this leadership position among the girls, it is going to be extra important that you show the way forward on this. This is an opportunity to show your friends how all of us should receive hard words. So while it sounds like you haven't been all that physical with the other girls, aren't the instigator in any case, and don't feel like you are anywhere near the heart of the problem, I still think it would be great for you to make it clear that you have been convicted, and that you intend to apply what we talked about.

Lead the way in acknowledging that you see a problem, and that you need to adjust some of your own behavior. This is one of those things where it may not have been a big deal when you were doing it last week (giving each other shoulder rubs all the time, sitting on each other's laps, etc.) because last week you were not noticing it. It was a thing that was becoming normal in your group, and as far as you knew there were literally no dangers involved. That's fine! But now that the Spirit has gotten your attention, it has become something that you have to deal with. To participate in that kind of behavior now would be to intentionally choose to behave foolishly. There is no upside to hardening your heart.

This is a little bit like drinking in college. There are a lot of people who drink for those four years, and then move on—it just ends up being a weird interlude in their life. But there are many other people who suffer long-term consequences: they come out of college as alcoholics. Similarly, most of you girls would probably have outgrown this handsy behavior and, in some ways, be none the worse—but that is simply not the case for all of you. This is an area where learning wisdom and growing up a bit will bless the entire group, and possibly a few particular girls more than the rest.

So this week I think you should focus on how you can lead in the physical tone of your group. Say something like, "Hey guys! I've been thinking about what we were talking about, and I think I've been acting foolishly, and I'm planning to stop. Will you forgive me?" Go ahead and give specifics if you have some.

In many Christian communities it has become uncommon for people to acknowledge petty sin and repent of it. But if you know there is forgiveness, then seeing your own sin is a wonderful mercy. You can thank God for rooting things out, and you can rejoice that you are growing. Remember that God disciplines those He loves. You are HIS! What a gift! So when you have a chance to do this, do it JOYFULLY! Do not make a big deal about it—just say that you don't want to act like a dummy anymore! Laugh at yourself, and cut yourself free of petty entanglements.

The freedom and joy of a clean conscience is a wonderful testimony—far, far more influential than pretending we never stumble or make stupid mistakes. So lead in joyful humility. It makes sense to me that you feel a little beat up. I didn't know I'd be stepping on your toes here, but the Lord clearly loves you. It is good that you have been feeling a burden for the problems these other girls seem to be having, and the best of all possible outcomes is that you are going to get to sort through a few of your own that you didn't see. We shouldn't want everyone else to get a better view of their sin, and then flinch when we get a better view of our own.

I'll be praying that this week will be really fruitful, and that God will bless those bits of leadership (and self-leadership) that are painful and uncomfortable. I'm proud of you!

Cheers,
Aunt Lizzie

LETTER 10

# Maturity

Dear girls,

I see from your comments that I should be clearer about a few things. Imagine with me that we are gardening together and struggling against a few types of massively invasive weeds. The kinds that spring up overnight and grow into a bush the size of your house with roots that require an excavator to dig out. I am wanting you all to recognize these weeds when they are still the size of your thumb. The idea is that if we pull them out now, we can do it with very little agony.

Recognizing little things that are growing into big things is an important part of maturity. When we see the little baby sins in our own lives, we should not defend and protect them just because they haven't had the afternoon to grow yet. The fact that they are little should make us more eager to yank them out, since we can do it with relatively little effort. I am not saying that any girl who has become handsy with others is currently in big weird sexual sin. But I am giving you a piece of wisdom that I have learned in my old age: Pull that weed out, now! This is not a plant you want to be growing.

I think you all would understand this easily if we were talking about some other kind of sin. Jesus says that if you hate someone, you have murdered them in your heart. He says that if you lust after someone, you have committed adultery with them in your heart. If you knew your mother was fantasizing about living alone in Italy, you might feel a little betrayed, and you'd be right: abandoning your family in your heart is not that far from abandoning your family in reality. The little things in our hearts are not actually little things in principle.

Let's get at this from another angle. If you had a habit of sneezing into your hand, someone might come up and say you should try sneezing into your elbow—that way you could more effectively end the germ spray and keep your hands clean. You would probably file their advice away as a random tip that might be handy. There would almost certainly be no emotions involved. It wouldn't cost you anything to entertain the possibility that they could be right.

Think of the advice in my last letter—keep your hands to yourself because literally no good will come of it—as a tip in this category. It shouldn't feel threatening or hurtful.

Now, if everything in you bridles against this and is outraged at what you perceive to be legalism—recognize that! For some reason, you are awfully invested in this behavior; this is more important to you than it should be. If you're compelled to defend a habit to the death, it's a good guess that the habit is unhealthy. You have developed a neediness that you should not nurture, or else a pride that won't let you admit you may have behaved foolishly.

This does not need to be a big deal for any of you. I'd suggest that you pray (individually) for the Lord to show you if your resistance here is godly or not. Ask Him to give you eyes to see your own behavior and to give you the courage to change, even if it feels embarrassing. Now, if you do not want to pray that—well then, you have another confirmation that this particular weed is getting deeper in your own life. Maybe you don't want to trust my input, and that's fine. But if you don't want to trust the Lord's input, then you have shown yourself that there's a little area of your life that you do not want the Lord to touch.

This is a little trick that I advise you to use frequently throughout your life. If something annoys you and you are kicking up all manner of arguments in your head about it, just stop that and pray: "Lord, I bring this to you. If it is something that I ought to be taking more seriously, please lay it on my conscience. Amen." It is a very healthy practice to immediately pursue the guidance of the Lord on anything like this. Ask Him. These are the sorts of prayers that the Lord loves to answer. One of the things you will find out almost immediately is that your defensive response is very often an unwillingness to consider truth. So when you feel yourself bridling up at something, consider it a little nudge. Put it on the altar. Offer it to God and let Him correct you.

There is something else that I would like to bring up today. Remember that you are all in the phase of life when you need to make your faith your own. You are coming out from under the shelter of your parents and your community; you're beginning to stand on your own two feet. In many ways you are learning to walk by faith for the first time because you are learning to walk *by yourself* in faith for the first time.

I hope that you can all remember learning to ride a bike. You sat with your feet on the pedals, your little hands squeezed around the tasseled handlebars, master of a new world. Your parents, meanwhile, were running behind you holding onto the seat in case of emergency.

This is a good picture of your current spiritual situation. You are riding the bike, yes, and you have not crashed in a little while. But your parents and your community are still providing a lot of the balance. Maturity starts by taking the *risks* seriously. Crashing and burning spiritually in your late teens has far worse consequences than some road rash. What's more, the consequences are only growing more deadly. The broader society outside of the church and family has removed all of the guardrails, and now there are whole industries actively pursuing the destruction of your life and soul. People are actually spending money on market research to learn how best to get at you.

But as is often the case, teens feel young and invincible! They are sure they are not going to fall. And so instead of acknowledging the risk and proceeding in a faith-filled and level-headed way, they start yelling (in a variety of ways—a lot can be said with an eye roll!) at the adults in their lives: "Oh my word! Leave me ALONE. I've got this totally handled, no problem, no concerns, and if you would only let go I could go straight down these concrete stairs and into the fountain at the bottom! Stop taking everything so seriously!"

Your parents do need to let go of you as you get older. But as they do, there are some simple things that you should be thinking about that will facilitate your maturity and build their trust. So here are a few suggestions, although this is not in any way an exhaustive list.

*1. Take some independent spiritual initiative.* You should be pursuing spiritual growth in ways that have not been laid out for you by those in authority over you. If you are already reading your Bible regularly, wonderful. If not, get serious about finding a way to make this part of your normal routine. This is going to be especially important if you have only ever done your Bible reading when your mother has organized it for you: given you the plan, checked in on your progress, scheduled a time for you to get it done. If the habit of Bible reading has not taken off in your life, you presumably have some obstacles to overcome. Overcome them! Set out to deal with them very frankly. Instead of looking at yourself through a filter that flatters you, turn on all the fluorescent lights and get a real eyeball full of whatever it is that's keeping you from the Word. Are you resisting reading your Bible because it annoys you that your mother wants you to do it? Is it because you wake up and check on social media, get busy with worldly concerns, and never even think about opening the Word? Is it because you find the Bible boring and don't think it is doing anything for you? Get an honest look at your temptations so you can begin the work of overcoming them. If you have not proven yourself capable of eating on your own, then you cannot be surprised or offended when people try to spoon-feed you. These sorts of problems are totally normal, but you will need to address them. You need to view yourself as an adult in the situation, and being a woman of the Word is one of your duties.

2. *Take clear responsibility for sin.* If you are convicted about something in your life, do not pretend you have not been. Just acknowledge it humbly and honestly and seek forgiveness from any who witnessed it. You should especially give some attention to what we could call domestic conflict. What are routine places or situations in your regular life where you are not a joy to be around? It is very likely that you rely on your parents to manage the situation at home (the attitudes and the squabbles, etc.). But if you need your mother to point out that you are being selfish or unkind or angry, then you really are not showing yourself to be mature. Learn to recognize when you're wrong, and then make it right. If you have consistently been in the wrong (general unkindness or snarky criticisms, cold-shouldering

the family, darting steely gazes around the room, shoving a sibling to get to the front seat), seek forgiveness for that. Tell whoever saw it that you should not have been behaving in that way, ask forgiveness as necessary, and in this way begin holding yourself to a higher standard.

3. *Ask for your parents' input on things that you need to work on.* What are the main areas that your parents think you need to mature in? And can you have that conversation with them without getting defensive or brittle? Pray in advance for a willing spirit to talk about it. Ask for their input, and even if you disagree with it, thank them and say you are going to pray about it (and then do!).

4. *Look for ways that you can serve in your church.* And really serve—find something that meets an actual need, something that you can simply offer to God, not just something to do socially. Is there an older widow who would appreciate someone coming by to clean her bathroom or visit with her? Every church has a lot of work that could be done, and a lot of work that has not already organized itself.

5. *Choose a skill that a grown woman ought to have that you do not, and take steps to learn it.* Expect this to take time and attention and work. I'm thinking of things like making a whole dinner for the family, baking a cake, sewing, or knitting, or baking good bread, etc. If there is something that you feel a little ashamed that you don't know how to do (maybe your friends know how to do it, and it feels awkward to acknowledge your lack), tackle that first. Make it a priority to do the work that it takes to learn it. Ask someone!

I believe that if you all work through these points, it will be like a sort of spiritual Miracle-Gro. If you manage to punch through this list in hardly any time, just go back through them all and do it again. There will always be more domestic skills to learn, more people to serve, more bad habits to fight.

Hoping you have a really busy week, full of stretching and growing and the very real joy that comes with that! Let me know how it goes!

Until next time,
Aunt Lizzie

LETTER 11

# Worldliness

Dear girls,

This week I thought of something that I should have already brought up with you, and I don't think I have. Consider this a sort of framing thought for the whole growing-up business you are undertaking.

If you look out over the vast sea of Christian women who are alive today, you will see many things that are not exactly encouraging. We live in an age of therapeutic rubbish, and a lot of diverse carnage has resulted from that. That carnage is plainly visible inside the church as well—you could easily go to a Bible study somewhere on how to follow your heart (never you mind that the Bible tells us explicitly not to do that). There are a lot of pitfalls out there, and nestled inside each one of them you can find an absolute tribe of women ready to receive you and welcome you into their little pool of unproductive and unfruitful and unfun yet (still professing) Christian lives.

So while I really hope that all of you know many Christian women that you admire and look up to, the church and the world at large desperately need your generation to outdo ours by a long way. You are in the difficult position of needing to behave in a more mature manner than many women twice your age. You ought to hold fast to truth, to expect a lot of yourselves, to dig your roots deeper into the Word and into your duties than you have seen done. Each generation should be able to stand on the shoulders of the generation before them. However, because of sin and foolishness and all of the consequences that come along with them, the human pyramid has fallen down. There are huge gaps. In many cases you might not see a pair of godly shoulders to stand on at all.

Many women in your mother's generation had this same experience. They were raised in daycare and public school while their mothers prioritized their careers. They really didn't have much firsthand knowledge to build on. In this I am not blaming anyone—each generation has had its outstanding achievers, and each generation has had its faithless underperformers. Many women have done extraordinarily well with difficult situations—like the parable, they were given little, but they invested it wisely.

Regardless of how exactly we got into this situation, we are coming up on a generational handoff where we need for you all to rise to the cultural occasion in a way that is exceptional and extraordinary. It needs to be something that has not really been seen before in history. And it needs to be done by real women, living lives empowered by the grace of God. I'm hoping that you are some of those women.

The temptation to join the world in its absolutely strength-destroying behavior is real. You are going to need to fight to keep yourself from being neutralized. There are a lot of people that want you to feel completely free to be a selfish, petty monster—not because they actually care that you are "seen and heard," or that you get the credit you think you deserve, or that you "boldly take up space," etc., but rather because they REALLY CARE that you not be strong enough to be a danger to their world. Encouraging selfishness is a great way to do that. If you're addicted to the world's praise or encouragement or affirmation, you'll be harmless enough and very easy to control.

Now when the Enemy comes around looking to mess you up, one of the things that he does *not* do is announce his intentions. He will not tell you that he is coming to take away your potential or your joy or your gratitude or your healthy relationships. Instead he will come to you in the guise of a giver: "I will empower you. I will help you be heard. I will make them notice you."

Do not—I cannot repeat this with enough force—*do not* give your strength away in such a cheap exchange. The moment that you let the Enemy's guidance into your life, you start losing the most valuable things. It is not ever worth it.

It is my prayer that my daughters and all of you wonderful young women in this generation will rise up as a force that no one saw coming. I know the Lord can do it, and I know that you all can be used mightily by Him. So stay the course, and set your mind on being faithful in the little things which will turn out to be more important than you ever imagined. Be open-handed, be strong, be courageous.

With love and also a lot of hope,
Aunt Lizzie

LETTER 12

# Messing Up

Dear girls,

What fun you've been having! I absolutely LOVED that list of all the new things you are trying to learn. I hope you will keep at it and see it through. It has always amused me how often women say something like "Oh I wish I knew how to knit!" Very rarely is this said by a person who will ever actually learn. It's not a secret people are keeping from you! Walk into any craft store (or even Walmart) and say, "I want to learn to knit," and someone can immediately show you the little section of beginning-to-knit supplies and directions. You could find a how-to-knit video in a hot second. There is nothing keeping anyone from this knowledge. But people who say things like this usually mean "I wish I was the sort of person who would learn how to knit." I recommend that you become that sort of person without spending years in the longing.

Get used to pushing yourself past the initial stagnation. For instance, the desire to learn to bake bread needs to actually walk into the grocery store, get the flour, and then go home and try it. Just put feet on your ideas and do things right away. Once you start, you'll usually discover more obstacles; your next goal should probably be "I want to learn to make better bread." But the thing is, you are actually going somewhere, and what is more, you are learning how to learn. You will have specific questions, and you can then get specific answers.

I have often joked that I could write a whole book on the spiritual lessons of crafting because the things you have to learn in order to succeed at these domestic arts are actually wildly helpful in spiritual matters too. It is a small theater in which you can learn some rather big life lessons. So you want to be a good hostess? You have to do more than say that or think that—you have to start taking steps in the real world to actually do it. This will build your understanding of how to do things, and you will begin to develop an intuition that can only be born of experience. The more you learn the better you get at learning. The more parties you actually throw, the more you notice what things you didn't do well. It will give you something else to work on right away, something else to troubleshoot and think about.

Back in college I decided to make bagels. I had baked things before, but I was definitely still in the "just do what the recipe says and be surprised at the result" stage. Anyways I pulled out a recipe for bagels and made them and they were *tremendously* bad. Rubbery, weird looking, sickly and grayish, not tasty, not cute, not nice, and full of weird little gummy bubbles—completely yuck.

I dismissed the recipe as a bad one to have led me so far astray. But somehow, at some point later, I was randomly convicted. What if—follow me closely—what if the fact that I was a novice baker and did not know what I was doing played into the outcome? What if the recipe was not as bad as I felt like it was? In a strange fit of baking godliness I made the same recipe for those bagels every day for at least a week. Guess what? By the end, the bagels were bagels I loved. Same recipe, different baker. Bagels are a good place to learn this sort of lesson because there are a lot of steps where things can go very wrong. That particular recipe had you broil them, boil them, and then bake them—and at every stage you seemed poised on the edge of ruining everything. Over the course of that week, I learned a lot of different ways to mess up a bagel before I figured out how to make a good one.

One of the most important things that you can do is learn to be good at being bad at things. Around the time of my great bagel-humbling, I remember realizing that, if I wanted to be an old lady who is good at a lot of things, then I would have to be a young lady who is good at being bad at them. You have to be willing to take on the "I am brand new at this and have no idea what I am doing" persona. It's not usually a flattering place to be.

When you fail at something that you wish you were good at—or hope that you will someday be good at—look at that failing as simply the first step to competence. The tricky thing about domestic arts is that many of us think of them as hobbies and not skills. Why would you keep working on a hobby if you don't enjoy it immediately? A skill is different. Take cake-decorating for example. You may not have the desire to haunt cake-decorating shops or work on icing flowers in all your spare moments. It might not be your hobby as you can see it is for others. But it is good to have the skills to do something sometime! Not because you will then take it up as a hobby, but rather because you might want to use a cake to tell your child you love them. Having different skills is like being able to communicate in different languages. It gives you a much broader range of tools to work with as you go about the real work of your life.

Several years ago (when I was wanting to get a potter's wheel), I watched a bunch of videos of people throwing bowls and pitchers and vases. Every video made it look smooth and effortless. It was not until I sat down with a big lumpy wad of clay that I realized what looked like ease was actually skill and experience.

So the first real skill to embrace is the joy of being bad at things, because it puts you on the path to being good at things. I tell my daughters that they are not allowed to say things that close doors on their future selves. I don't care if you don't embroider and your sister does—you won't go around saying "I can't" and mentally consigning yourself to a life of inability. Just because you do not take as naturally to something does not mean that you cannot learn and excel at it. There are many things that I love and enjoy doing that I was not good at right away. Some of the things I'm best at took some of the most embarrassing plot points to learn. I am still consistently bad at new things. But I am also consistently getting better at things that aren't so new anymore. I cannot think of anything that I have applied myself to learn that I could say in retrospect was a waste of time—even if it is not a thing that I still do. So don't be easily discouraged by a little expectable failure! And don't think that everything you do has to have a long-term strategic destination. You learned math with a lot of worksheets—the domestic arts simply use more than paper to learn on, and some waste is to be expected. Besides making you a more interesting person, learning how to do a thing is so good for your brain and your self-discipline that it is worth the time no matter the result.

When my kids were little and would frequently turn the house into a complete disaster in minutes, I used to gather them up and talk with them about using their hands for "good instead of evil." Imagine I have gathered you all up right now in the same way. Look around the room at all of you! How many hands are there in this room? How much good could be done with those hands in one week? What kind of a difference could you make in this world if each of you learned to use your hands very capably to make beautiful meals, to keep beautiful homes, to steward spaces and ingredients and fabric and yarn to the glory of God and the good of others? As you figure out new ways to bless those around you (by the way, I LOVE your speed-cleaning group idea—I hope you find many opportunities to bless your church with that!) you will notice that you are becoming more and more capable. You will have eyes to see needs that you were not previously looking for. And because you are not afraid to try and to learn new things, huge horizons really will open up. If you aren't afraid to try things you don't already know how to do, you will be far more willing to try to meet the needs that you can see.

Think big for a moment. If you all keep learning and growing and pursuing creative efforts and acts of service, how much good could all of your hands do over the course of twenty years? Even better—how many hands capable of serving and building and loving are represented in this room if you all go on to be the mothers of many? Take advantage of this time. When you are a grandmother looking around your dining room table at the people who were very much your life's work, will you, at that point, wish you had spent more time on social media or shopping or just sitting around gossiping? Will you wish you had taken a few more selfies but this time more flattering? Will you wish you had had a photographer friend so you could have gotten more pictures of yourself in exceedingly trendy poses, clothes, and locations? Get busy now trying to be the kind of women that you want to be then. Get busy learning to be the kind of women who are the matriarchs of great families.

It sounds like you are all off to the races already, and I am so glad. There are few things more fruitful than young women throwing themselves into the domestic arts. Oh to live up to the wonderful blessing in Deuteronomy 28:5: "Blessed shall be your basket and your kneading bowl."

One other thing while I am on this topic—learning things together provides a very healthy structure for your friendships. Practice what I would call "shoulder-to-shoulder friendship," where the point of the friendship is not gazing at each other or gossipping, but rather enjoying something else. You are all pursuing a common goal in the ultimate sense, but you are also hopefully pursuing smaller ones. Learn new skills together, and talk with each other about things that you are learning. Do not make it a habit to "hang out" with no particular goal or purpose. In such circumstances the temptation to gossip or dabble in vain and idle behavior becomes almost unavoidable—and you begin to structure your friendships and thought life all around the shallowest things possible.

In some ways, working together can seem shallower than you expected friendship to be. How could it be that learning to make pie crust or donuts or cheese or really any domestic skill or art could be a deeper and realer thing to do than sitting around talking about how you are feeling? It does seem counterintuitive, but I can tell you from a lifetime of experience that doing things together goes far deeper than a stagnant time of reflection. When you start trying things, you uncover a lot about yourself—including things you may not like to see. It turns out that there is adversity in pies. There are lessons to learn and trials to endure. True, it is all in a little small arena—scorched there on the bottom of the oven and smoking out the kitchen. But that is what is so good about it. He who is faithful with a little will be faithful with much. There are so many spiritual lessons and challenges that new skills require. Even as I write this I am sitting in the same room with my floor loom, which I love, and which has upon it a project I have *not* loved for way too long. I am much older than you, and I'm still needing to learn to persevere and finish something that did not go as smoothly as I had first hoped, but is still worth finishing.

Another benefit to getting your friendships forward-facing is that you can be far more inclusive. You have something to talk about that is broadening yourselves. When you meet someone that you do not have much in common with, you have something to invite them to join you in. In *The Four Loves*, C.S. Lewis says that those who are going nowhere can have no fellow travelers. This should be your life friendship slogan. DO SOMETHING FRUITFUL and enjoy the company of those who come along with you.

Many years ago now, my oldest daughter was having a bad time at recess because no one was playing with her. She was sad about it—and as the mother of this poor little kindergartener, I was feeling sorry for her! But then I asked her what she was doing at recess, and she revealed that she was just standing on the playground (presumably grieved in her spirit). I asked her, why would anyone want to come feel sorry for her with her? There was nothing at all to do there!

So the next day, I gave her an assignment: scoop a bowl in the pea gravel and forage ingredients to make "soup." I told her not to ask anyone to play—just make soup. When she came home the next day, recess had been fun. Tons of fun. I asked her what the other kids did while she made soup, and she said, "Oh they all did it with me."

There is no reason that your own friendships cannot follow this pattern in a more mature way. Since your group is quite big, I am sure there are little subgroups within it. And I am sure there are subgroups that some of you wish you could be part of. There is a weird temptation in this natural situation to make the other people the goal: "All I want is to get into that group where I can go sit in her car and drink coffee and laugh at whatever it is that they are always laughing about." Doing this is, to be completely frank, dumb. It opens you up to temptations that you really shouldn't get tangled up in. Instead of standing on your life playground feeling sorry for yourself, make a goal. Be interested in things. Learn new skills. You will be surprised by the friendship opportunities that will simply appear as you work on things that are worth doing for their own sake. People can sense it when you have interests that are not them (you are not needy!), which makes it way more inviting and interesting and less fraught with emotional hazards to hang out with you. Loaded friendships are no fun—you can feel the entangling expectations in the air. But when you are clearly invested in figuring something out, that is far (*far!*) more inviting. It feels worlds less needy and less dangerous.

I suppose you could compare friendship to barbeque. There are some meats that you want to cook over a very hot fire, directly facing the heat. But a lot of meats work much better in indirect heat, where they can be cooked low and slow. Friendships are like that. Going into a friendship too hot and too fast results in friendship burnouts. You simply cannot maintain it for a long time. My great-grandma used to give a piece of wisdom that is worth living by: Get to know everyone first, then choose your friends. Do not pull a "desperate for friends" move on anyone who gets into your line of sight. Work on other things, think about other things, and get to know people when the focus is not directly on getting to know each other. If you feel like someone is coming in a little hot, it is wise to change the intensity of the heat right off the bat. Give the hanging out a purpose, give it a time frame, and probably get a few other people in there too.

I can't wait to hear the updates on how all of this goes for you all! Maybe sometime soon I can make an aspirational list of things that I think are good for any young woman to know how to do. I have been wanting to do that for my own girls. With four daughters, I need a list just to make sure I've taught everyone the same things!

Until next time,
Aunt Lizzie

LETTER 13

# Tastemaking

Dear girls,

It wasn't until high school that I really took the plunge into any of the domestic arts. I certainly had been around them. My older sister (older by four years) liked to sew—she was on a bender of sewing her own jeans at the time. My mother also sewed a lot, and had done some knitting as a teenager. At one point, she even had a loom in our house.

But I played volleyball and basketball and ran track, and for me, the fabric store represented something other people did. I remember looking in true horror at the assorted patterns of dolls you could crochet to cover a

Kleenex box, clowns you could make out of fabric yo-yos, and many more terrifying crafts. It was shockingly easy to make fun of, and that was mostly what I did.

But around this time, I was struck by all the beautiful things we had that my grandmother had made, and my great-grandmother, and even my great-great-grandmother. All of a sudden I imagined myself handing these heirlooms on to my children, and then having to say something like "But I never really did anything. Nothing to show from me."

Of course I do not believe that having handmade things to give your children is the most important thing you can possibly do. But it is really healthy to think like this. It is good and right to look beyond yourself and this week's problems. It is good and right to think instead about the generations coming next. One of my girls has a beautiful afghan that was crocheted by her great-great-grandmother. How happy Granny would be if she saw where that project ended up! Draped over the knees of a girl four generations away from her, reading a novel and eating an apple.

Learning to make beautiful things that will bless the people around you (and build your house) is in itself a beautiful thing. No matter what the project ends up looking like, it is an inheritance. The things you make don't have to be heirlooms—in fact many projects don't do well with such a burden put on them. But they are part of the inheritance that your life and faithful work will be to them anyways.

So back to my situation as a high schooler. For the first time, I noticed that I knew how to do nothing that would create anything worth passing on. I wanted to change that.

I also realized that I wanted to have some ability (however moderate) in a lot of different areas. I wanted to be able to make the things that I needed and not just be stuck in one craft when I wanted to be creative. That is how I imagine we got the crochet-doll Kleenex cover in the first place. Someone only knew how to do one craft but desperately wanted to make *something*. There comes a time when there are not many more things to crochet that you actually want, so you have to start crocheting things that you don't really want and no one has ever wanted. It's only a theory, but I think I can see how this sort of thing happens. I've made some terrible things myself in this way—being swept up in a technique or idea that did not pan out to be beautiful. Don't limit yourself to one creative outlet. Live creatively!

One time, I knit a wool sweater in a bulky yarn (with TWO strands held together). It was the world's most claustrophobic sweater: unbearably hot and about four times less comfortable than anything else I have ever worn. Knowing I couldn't manage to wear it more than that one terrible time, I decided to try felting it and turning it into a bag. (You do this by washing the wool in hot water so that it thickens up and turns into solid fabric.) It felted right up into something that looked like a fire hydrant! It stood up by itself in the alley by our trash can. Some things are best handed down only as a warning and a funny memory.

The important thing in all of this is to start broad and spend time getting to know what sorts of things are possible. One way to do this is to spend time asking yourself why you think something is beautiful—or how you might fix something that you think is ugly. For example, maybe you dislike the quilts you have seen at a quilt show or a fair. Why? What is it that you don't like specifically, and is there anything that you *do* like in what you see? If you were making a quilt, how would you avoid what you don't care for and achieve what you do?

You can do the same thing for interior design. When you walk into a room, what do you notice? What are the characteristics of spaces you like to be in? Why? Try to put a finger on what you like or don't like—what you think works in a space and what doesn't. Pay attention! Look deeper than just the surface. If someone put you in charge here what would you change? If the space isn't comfortable, what would make it feel more natural? This is a very low-key and informal way to put yourself through a training regime. What do you like about the way this meal is put together or presented? How does it look on the plate? These are not idle thoughts or questions. You are shaping your imagination. You are figuring out what you ought to learn and do.

Your eventual home will be an expression of the things that you love. You have to build up your own imagination about what that home should be like. What do you love most or feel is homiest about your own home? Having a clear idea on these things will equip you to manage your work later because you will already have an idea of what you are aiming for, as well as some ability to troubleshoot what isn't working. This will give you a great head start.

It is much easier to get right down to the work of your life when you already know what you like and what you are aiming for. It is not at all uncommon for girls to assume that beautifying your house will just be the work of a moment, but it actually isn't. Homes have an animating character in them—a woman who needs to be making decisions and acting on them.

You may know that you like the style of one particular store, but it is fairly unlikely that you will start out as a newlywed with the financial resources to simply order whatever you like. On top of that, when you get married you will be merging the things that you like and enjoy with the things that your husband likes and enjoys. It is much easier to do this well when you are well-versed in the subject in the first place. It is not uncommon for women who have spent no time thinking about this sort of work to end up needing a lot of help and support from their husbands. But this is a uniquely feminine job, and it should be a delight for women to know more about it than their husbands. You should be bringing a whole field of knowledge and understanding that he has never considered. This is one of the many ways that you can be a tremendous blessing to your future husband and your future children—by providing the comfort of a well-thought-out and well-loved home without them having to think through it all.

Honestly all of this could be filed under the heading "Make hay while the sun shines." Being the mistress of a productive, fruitful, and beautiful home requires you to make decisions, be confident in what you want, and accomplish the goals that you have set for yourself. You will need practice at all of these things, and the sooner you start, the better. You will not always have the bandwidth and time that you do now! So be hungry to learn. Read cookbooks and homemaking books. Try recipes and try them again. Try the basics of as many different skills as you can. Do you know what it takes to paint a bookshelf or freshen up a lamp? These are things you can do on a small scale in your own bedrooms, now. Get practice in as many things as possible. Then hone in on the things that you especially enjoy or think are beautiful and learn more about those. Do not assume that you will have time later. Instead, get yourself into a lifetime habit of learning and growing. This is a fundamental skill that you will take with you into the rest of your life, and it will be a great blessing to you and to all the people around you.

One small caution: Do more than watch other people do things well. Cooking shows make things look easy and smooth. The same is true for interior decorating shows and crafting videos. But trying something yourself will teach you a lot more than watching someone else do it. You can become knowledgeable about something without developing much capability in it at all. Do not simply turn into a critic, holding your mother or someone else's baking ability up to the cookbook you looked at once.

You might think that reading broadly and always evaluating spaces and meals seems arrogant. And it certainly can be if that is as far as you ever take yourself. The reality is that nothing is more humbling than trying to do things and seeing the shortfalls in your own work.

Now I'm sure some of you are thinking that I am vastly overrating the importance of the domestic arts. It doesn't seem like such a complicated job. Why get into a big swizzle over learning things that no woman you know has used, much less needed in her home? In some ways you are not wrong. But Scripture calls women to be "keepers at home," and I am simply wanting to see a generation of women who put some elbow grease into it. We have lost so much culturally in this area through the generations, and the work of restoring that knowledge has to come through specific women giving themselves to it with more joy and enthusiasm than the generation before them did. While the footholds on this particular path are little and unimportant when taken alone, the journey certainly isn't.

When women value their work and pursue excellence in it, God uses it in ways that you just can't see on the surface. This is how culture is built. This is how you raise the bar for the next generation. This is how you make your home a place that your children want to be. This is also how you glorify your husband's labor by turning your home into an expression of all that the both of you hold dear and believe.

A husband and a wife have different roles and callings—and when all is going well and rightly between them, their roles weave together into one very strong family unit. Scripture says that a husband is to imitate Christ, loving sacrificially and providing for his family. The wife, on the other hand, is to imitate the church, submitting joyfully and expressing her husband's love to the world. Now imagine a truly hard-working, high-achieving husband who loves his family and wants to care for them. But then imagine that his wife is really dropping the ball. She doesn't know how to set a table or make a meal. She doesn't know how to make the home a nice place to be. No matter how competent that man is at being a man, he is crippled in expressing his love to his family. He is crippled in the contribution that his household can make in building the kingdom.

Take that same man and give him a capable, competent, and joyful wife. When he comes home and she has made dinner and the family gathers around the table—what exactly is happening? He is able, through her faithful work, to express his physical love and care for his family. His labor now tastes like something and looks like something; it can be enjoyed in a way that just a paycheck never could. His work has taken on a personality. A wife glorifies her husband's work by turning it into real things that can be felt and seen and tasted. He gets to enjoy the tangible expression of his love for her and the children, and her love in response. She takes his work at the office and turns it into the blessing of clean socks, cozy beds, and filling meals.

When a husband and wife are in harmony, working hard in their own fields and enjoying the fruit of each other's work, the result is a powerful home, full of love and tangible joy. This is a home that will taste good, and look good, and feel like a safe and joyful place to be. And this is simply not the kind of thing that happens without a woman who throws herself into the many different tasks and skills and plain old elbow grease that make up a home.

Homemaking also happens to be (and I really cannot emphasize this part enough) the most absolutely FUN job in the world. It's hard and challenging for sure. Obstacles abound. It's stressful at times, and it can be a real uphill battle. But it is also a job with tremendous freedom. In an age that values entrepreneurship as much as ours does, it is a marvel that being a homemaker is still not admired. There are few occupations that allow for such freedom of self-starting enterprise as that of homemaker—and yet in common parlance it is still filed under the category of "not working."

Now I am saying this to a group of girls that I know are being educated and educated well. I do not think homemaking skills are more important than being well-read, being a thinker, being someone who can follow an argument and engage with philosophical ideas. But in circles like ours where education is already valued, we need to press in and learn to value the domestic arts as a uniquely feminine manifestation of a well-educated, well-disciplined, loving, generous, and FREE mind. I'm not saying you don't need the formal education you are receiving—if you were only learning how to sew and knit, I would be urging you to read some history too, and not neglect the life of the mind. But I know that your parents have already invested themselves in getting you a good education, and have sacrificed much to do so. That is a tremendous gift, one that you will have many opportunities later in life to appreciate more than you already do now.

I'm still going to work on that list of skills for you—you can expect it next week! But for this week's discussion I would like to encourage each of you to answer these questions.

1. When have you been to a meal (in any home or in any restaurant) that seemed really exceptional in some way? Was it fun, comforting, inspiring, beautiful? Try to pinpoint what made it that way and why. This could be really little details! Were the drinks in glass bottles? Were the napkins pretty and nice to touch? Was the lighting different? Was it more casual than you expected, or more elaborate? When you know what it was that made the meal really fun, make up a scenario where you might use those same tricks to accomplish a similar thing.

2. Think of a space you have been in that you love, and ask yourself why. Is it super inviting and comfortable? What makes it that way? How could you apply this elsewhere? What about a space that you felt should have been amazing but for some reason wasn't?

This is like learning to look at brushstrokes in a painting. You can know that you like the whole thing without looking close enough to see how it was accomplished. But if you have any desire to be a painter yourself, the brush strokes are very important! Try to cultivate a habit of looking and asking and thinking and remembering.

Until next time,
Aunt Lizzie

# LETTER 14

# Drama

Dear Lottie,

I am so pleased to hear all these fabulous reports! It sounds like you are having a ton of fun together. I really don't think anything could be healthier than focusing your friendships on working and learning rather than the "search your souls" gathering. Definitely do that trip to the library together—that was a fun idea of your mom's! I'm sure you can find some very dated books on design or food. Out-of-fashion books are great for kicking you right out of the world of Instagram and Pinterest or anything else that is so curated for right this minute. Don't merely be horrified by what you find. Look for principles that are still working, look for some takeaway insights or good ideas, ask yourself how you would change something to make it attractive. It is very tempting to laugh at the styles of the past without seeing how many dated styles we have today. You too will someday have children who are not able to believe the things you thought were cool!

I always advise people to learn to knit on a dishcloth. It's my favorite first project because you can get the basics, get a little practice, and then be done with it and have something useful. Dishcloth cotton (usually called "Peaches and Cream" or "Sugar and Cream") is the cheapest yarn anyways, so the investment is low. In my opinion, clover bamboo circular knitting needles (16 inches, size 7 or 8) are the absolute best to learn on. They are not too slippery and not too pointy, and they are attached to one another, which keeps them under control and in your lap while you work. Plus, they are sold in lots of places that regularly have coupon sales on them. I used to keep my dishcloth knitting in the glove box of the car to help fill any moment I was just sitting and waiting. It felt like dishcloths were just falling from heaven—I could not believe how much I could get done in the time that nothing was happening! After a while, one of my young children referred casually in conversation to the passenger seat of the car as "the knitting seat"!

Many people begin with glorious intentions to make a scarf or a blanket. The trouble is that the project is too big to finish quickly at the same skill level you began it. Unless you are some kind of a prodigy, it will not look super professional when you start. This is a much more liveable problem in a dishcloth. I remember fondly one of my college roommates choosing for her first project a school bus yellow scarf. At one end, it had unexpected holes and waved in and out in width—and then suddenly, it evened out and went along smoothly for a few inches until, as if from nowhere, a cable erupted in the middle of it and ran to the end. That project turned out to be more of a learning sampler!

Anyways, I would recommend you start with the dishcloths. Our favorite patterns are easily found online: Grandmother's Favorite is the best to start with since it is all one color. Even after you have the basic knit stitch figured out, knitting one of these is still interesting because you will increase and decrease (and obviously learn how to do both of those things). One final plus about Grandmother's Favorite is that the garter stitch texture works well for wiping tables and counters. If anyone gets overly ambitious, you can make this pattern into a baby blanket pretty easily by simply knitting much longer before beginning the second half with decreases. After you've mastered Grandmother's Favorite, I would recommend Clover Tweed, which is done in two colors with slip stitches. It's fun to make, and it looks very sharp when it's finished. I also like the Ball Band Dishcloth and the Linoleum Dishcloth. Linoleum is a more elaborate two-color cloth (but the favorite of my daughters), and Ball Band uses some slipped stitches and purl rows to make a multicolor brick-wall-like pattern. There's a version where you do the last couple bands in a new color, making it a three-color pattern—very fun to knit. All of these patterns make beautiful gifts, and are a joy to use.

There is nothing very difficult about learning to knit. Almost every pattern will have a key for the abbreviations it uses, and a quick Google will take you to abounding tutorials for any step you may not know how to do. I have always done English-style knitting (also called throwing), but you could learn Continental if that appeals to you or feels more natural. If you get in a pickle, I'm happy to help. I moonlight occasionally as an emergency knitting consultant. There is an old rhyme which can be helpful in remembering the steps of the knit stitch: "In through the front door, all around the back—out through the window, and off jumps Jack!"

I can't pass up this opportunity to impart some street-smart laundry tips to you. Dishcloths should be fresh every day. Whenever they are used, they should be rinsed and hung on the edge of the sink or over the faucet, not left in a wad in the corner with some old food and water to foster a clammy bacteria colony. When you're ready to clean them, hang them to dry somewhere first (I put them on the edge of a wire basket in the laundry room) instead of tossing them into the laundry basket where they will perpetrate evil and do no good. I wash my dry crunchy dishcloths in a batch on hot and always have a stash of nice cheerful clean ones to use.

Now to your question about those friends who have gone on a different path. It seems like the problem you are having now is not with the deconstructors, but rather with the girls who feel bad for moving on from them.

The quick answer is that no, it is not ungodly or unhealthy that you have moved on and are having a lot of fun doing things that are infinitely less angsty than those first few weeks were. In fact, it's really good. It's a sign of health and godliness that your friend group is not being dominated by those two girls' disobedience. We tend to have a lot of unnecessary ideas about what friendship is, and those assumptions really come out to play when this kind of conflict happens. Biblically speaking, friendship is not an evangelism tool. Of course we should be kind and generous to everyone, but when we are choosing our friends, Scripture says we should be careful:

> The righteous should choose his friends carefully, For the way of the wicked leads them astray. (Prov. 12:26)
>
> Do not be deceived: "Evil company corrupts good habits." (1 Cor. 15:33)
>
> Make no friendship with an angry man, and with a furious man do not go, Lest you learn his ways and set a snare for your soul. (Prov. 22:24–25)

We are supposed to choose our friends wisely and cautiously. Let's say two of you with different standards are listening to music together. Unless you fight over every song choice, the lowest standard will become the shared standard. If you're listening to music that's full of debauch, it doesn't matter that someone else chose it, or that it's only coming up every other song. You are still consuming it. You can't listen to a song without listening to it. You can't watch a show without watching it. That's just not the way it works.

Of course friendship is, and can be, a sanctifying relationship. Go back to that same hangout situation and imagine one friend saying to the other, "What on earth? This is a terrible song! You don't believe this! What is it doing on your playlist?" In a healthy friendship these sorts of incidents occur along the way and are resolved. But what must not happen is the slow compromise of people who fear conflict.

Your situation is awkward because we are talking about girls who you would have called friends in years past. But it is important to note that you have not moved—they have. If they wanted to come back into fellowship with you all, you would welcome them. You are simply refusing to go with them elsewhere. They have decided to wander, and you have decided to stay put.

As for the girls who feel like hanging out with them is ministering to them, I would simply disagree. By giving them an audience and clustering around them at every opportunity, they are making their disobedience rewarding. It reminds me of the opening of *The Silver Chair,* where Lewis describes the school leaders who are so entranced by the psychology of bad behavior that the bullies become a sort of teacher's pet. This happens all the time—and this is what is happening here. It is a bad idea for more than one reason. Just notice how these "tenderhearted" girls are cutting themselves off from all of their faithful friends to give themselves over almost entirely to girls who are trying to walk away from the faith. This is unhealthy, and it is also almost certainly not going to be effective. This kind of attention works as an incentive and not a disincentive. It rewards stupid sin by turning the sinner into a minor local celebrity. All a girl has to do is say she is doubting her faith, and then just wait to be fawned over and have people bring her coffees for no reason.

When our girls were in elementary school, we got the opportunity to talk about these classic female roles because they typically make themselves known on the playground. There's the girl who gets a mood or a 'tude or a hurt feeling and theatrically goes to cry behind the bus—she wants everyone to know what she's doing. Then there's some offender or a group of offenders who might be playing tag or jump rope or doing any manner of other things (except noticing the tears). And then, universally, there's also a third character or group of characters who take it upon themselves to channel the hurt feelings around. They are the ambassadors of emotions. They carry messages back and forth, and basically make their entertainment at recess the feelings of others and the related conflict. They love to deliver the news of why someone is mad at someone else, what might make her feel better, and many more such things.

This is not a game you should be playing. Resist the temptation to get into dramatic interpersonal situations. If you have sinned against someone, get it right. But if someone is making themselves a source of emotional entertainment whenever possible, run. This is not a healthy pastime. The girls who assume the role of middleman in every bout of tears are indulging something that they would do far better to resist. Whenever you feel the urge to talk to a friend about someone else's troubles, ask yourself whether you're part of the problem or part of the solution. If you're neither, then you're probably indulging in gossip. The difficulty with these middlemen is that they think they are part of the solution when they are really part of the problem.

This is called triangling. It is easy to be drawn in because it is flattering. When someone confides in you that they are struggling with someone else, it feels good! "I am the angel of mercy," (you think) "without whom this poor soul would be trapped in difficulty." The problem is that allowing yourself to be drawn into other people's emotional problems does not actually help them. People tend to triangle when they are anxious—too anxious to just deal directly with the conflict. When you are brought into a situation like this, you may end up stuck, because you cannot actually deal with a conflict that has nothing to do with you. All you're really doing is enjoying your friend's anxiety. But in surprising contrast, when you refuse to be drawn in, you *can actually help* by encouraging the other person to shoulder responsibility for their own problem.

Refusing to be drawn in is not unkind and does not require rudeness. But it does require courage. It is not easy, and it can feel very counterintuitive socially. My Grandma Bessie had a trick for handling these sorts of situations. Whenever someone came to her with a story of how someone else was wronging them (typically under the guise of needing counsel from her), she would sometimes say, "Wow, these are very serious accusations. I'll go with you now to confront her."

As you can imagine, the person in this situation never took Grandma Bessie up on her offer. They just wanted to spread the anxiety, not end it. In the same vein, a trick that my Grandpa Jim liked to use was to write out the accusations that someone unloaded on him, and then ask them to sign it. People rarely want to deal with their problems in this straightforward kind of a way.

To bring this all around to your current situation, just ask yourself some perfectly clear questions and answers. Have you been unkind to anyone? No. Should you be pursuing friendship with girls who have shown that they are not interested in pursuing godliness? Also no. Do these girls know that they are welcome back as soon as they decide that they do want to pursue godliness? Yes, it sounds like you have made that totally clear to them. If you feel like you haven't been perfectly clear, then you could consider writing them a letter in which you make sure to touch on the important points. A letter can be helpful because it is not an argument, and it can be read more than once. Writing a letter would also mean that, when you run into them, you can simply be kind rather than feeling at all moments like you need to express disapproval. Get it on the record and then don't worry about it.

In situations like this, it's easy to get stuck in a vortex of doubts. But doubts are frequently "what ifs"—and what ifs don't have answers. What if we handled their rebellion the wrong way? What if they feel like we don't care, since we are all happily doing other things now? What if they would repent if I started hanging out with them all the time? There aren't actual answers to these questions, and mulling over them never did anyone any good.

Feel free to share this with anyone in the group—I'll leave that up to you to decide if it would be helpful!

Cheers!
Aunt Lizzie

LETTER 15

# Homemaking

Dear girls,

The long-awaited list is giving me more trouble than I expected. As it turns out, it could easily become an encyclopedia. I am just going to give some major highlights. You should definitely feel free to scratch out one thing and put in another. This list is intended to give you ideas, but not to give you the idea that if you can do all these specific things, then you will be a godly wife. Also, I am not suggesting that you need to master every one of these skills—just that you should have a working knowledge of what they require and some experience trying your hand at them. Of course the more skills the merrier! You will never have a reason to regret being a more capable, more interesting person, so you really don't want to be aiming for the lowest common denominator. Aim high! Add to the list!

## Cooking:

- Roast chicken & a basic gravy (and sides!)
- Roast beef & gravy & a side
- Soup from scratch—a creamy soup, a broth soup, a whole chicken soup . . .
- Lasagna
- Enchiladas
- Homemade pasta (rustic noodles for the soup would be a good place to start)
- A pasta dish
- Chili
- Stir fry of some kind
- Rice, polenta, couscous (the cheapest filling side starches!)
- Roasted veg
- Steak or chicken or fish in a skillet with a pan sauce
- Tacos, or a good burrito
- Salad dressing (a simple vinaigrette!)
- Pork for shredding
- A simple jam
- Fresh salsa

# Baking:

- Quick bread (like banana)
- Sweet bread (like cinnamon rolls)
- Muffins
- Scones
- Cookies
- Cake
- Brownies
- Sandwich bread
- A peasant bread
- Dinner rolls
- Pie
- Quiche
- A fruit crumble or cobbler or crunch
- A laminated dough! Danishes or croissants, etc.

# Handwork:

- Sewing on a button
- The basics of a sewing machine
- A quilt block
- Sew a throw pillow
- How to knit
- How to crochet
- How to embroider
- Paint something

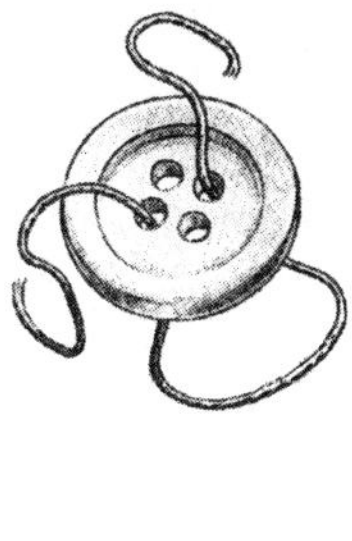

## Other:

- How to set a table
- How to plan a menu
- How to shop at the grocery store
- How to clean a bathroom
- How to make a bed
- How to do laundry
- How to iron a shirt

In this list (especially the cooking portion!) you should be trying to figure out how to make the version of each item that you like best. My family has our favorite muffins, for example, and those are the ones that I make. Make the things you want to eat most! Once you've done that, there probably won't be many recipes that intimidate you. You don't need to have made every variation of something before you know "how to do it."

Along the way, keep your eyes open for techniques you can apply or adapt in other places. From one recipe you may learn the trick of thickening the pasta sauce with a little of the pasta water—and that may be a technique that you use when you are making a random pasta sauce out of the things you find in the fridge.

Learning how to do one version of a thing will give you the skills to handle a much larger genre of things. You may not need to make anything gluten-free or dairy-free for your family. But if you know how to roast a chicken and veg and make a crisp, you will be able to minorly adapt to vegan butter and gluten-free flour and have a lovely meal to offer someone with a more exclusive diet.

One of my long-term goals has been to be able to know what to do with any given piece of meat without consulting a recipe. I'll be working on this forever probably, and I recommend it as a fun and interesting side quest. If you pay attention to the principles that appear in each recipe you use, you will start to have an intuitive knowledge of temperatures and seasonings and why you are sautéing some ingredients before other ones. Searing your roast first does actually make it much more tasty.

In other words, don't just stare at a recipe. Pay attention to the thing you are doing. This kind of thinking teaches you to troubleshoot, which will give you a real head start in the kitchen, as well as life in general.

Now girls, if you looked at this list and realized you pretty much know how to do most of it—that is wonderful! But don't start coasting. You haven't "arrived." And if any of you saw this list and hated me for it, feeling like you haven't learned how to do anything yet—DO NOT be discouraged! All this means is that there are a great many things waiting for you that will give you and those around you a lot of joy. Everything that I have mentioned is something that can be enjoyed by more than one person. These are tools of community- and culture-building. As you begin to master them, you are equipping yourself to pull people together, to build something beautiful, and to bless people with the work of your hands and your imagination.

As much as the world would like to tell you that learning to cook and clean is learning to be a drudge of some kind, it's just a blatant falsehood. Knowing how to make a home that people want to live in and to lay a table that people want to eat at is empowering in the best kind of way. This is not the work of a drudge. A home is the place where people are made—where people come together to share meals (and meals are about far more than just fueling up). Homemakers have a rather unlimited level of influence. Of course, there are drudge-like elements to the job. It is actually hard work. Even if you really enjoy making a beautiful meal, you probably would prefer to do so at a much slower pace than life requires. But here is the thing: there are many drudge-like moments in *any* important work. You could be in charge of an incredible and excellent company, and your work would still have its moments of being incredibly work-like.

You know the famous old quote: "The hand that rocks the cradle is the hand that rules the world." Raising children is a wild privilege that is absolutely critical for the preservation of any society. The hand that rocks the cradle is not the hand of a mere nanny, and it's doing a lot more than just rocking a cradle.

The home has been under so much attack because it is unbelievably strategic. In any war, supply lines are a target. You do not want your enemy feeding and encouraging the troops, training new troops, and keeping morale high. If I were the Devil, targeting women is one of the most effective things that I could think of doing. Get women to quit, and the joy goes out of the home. Without a joyful woman, the home fires stop burning. And without that force, the home loses the power it has to strengthen, encourage, and shape both the current generation and the up-and-coming one. When you go after a mother, you can get at multiple generations in one blow. Of course, the next best thing to getting a woman out of the home is to keep her in it with a withering attitude.

Scripture says that a wife who causes shame is "rottenness in her husband's bones," which is pretty much fatal. But a woman who faithfully fears the Lord is a "crown of glory" on her husband. You can be your husband's fatal cancer or you can be his crown. I am in favor of you all getting the training you need to be the most glorious, most effective, and most powerful wives that you can possibly be: the mothers of multitudes, the makers of culture, the remakers of civilization.

To be clear (and this point is very important), it will very rarely feel like what I have just described. I've said before that faithfulness usually does not feel like anything great—and this is one of the reasons that women need to be resilient and strong. It is hard to keep your eyes on what is actually happening when there are a lot of bothersome distractions. You can miss the joy of the family around the table because you had a sleepless night and are only seeing the dishes that will have to be done. Your feelings are not automatically tuned to the reality of the situation before you. This is one of the most persistent temptations that homemakers and mothers face: to give in to the feelings that their work is not important, that it isn't making a difference, that it is *meaninglessly* repetitive and dull. There will be lots of attacks on your morale because, in many ways, women are the morale of the family.

There's an old blues song that says "When Mama ain't happy, ain't nobody happy." This is actually a pretty accurate statement, as I am sure some of your own life experience tells you. When you were a little kid and you came home and the house felt alive and warm and joyful, and there was good food to eat, and it smelled nice, what did that do for your soul? I remember this feeling very clearly myself—it was so relieving to come home after a long day of school. When Mom treats her work like drudgery, everyone feels it as exactly that, but when she is full of joy, it seems like everything she does is an encouragement.

When I was in high school I started a hand-pieced baby quilt using the English paper-piecing method (where you baste a bunch of one-inch hexagons around larger paper hexagons and then sew them together). I started it impulsively. I remember joking about maybe being done in time for a grandbaby. I thought I was wildly exaggerating, but I was apparently more intuitive than funny: the project still is not done, and grandbabies (Lord willing) are not so far off on the horizon. Anyways, every once in a while I pull it out and work on it a little more. This last spring break I took it with me to the Oregon Coast, at which time my daughters (all four teens!) jumped into helping with it. It was not planned, but they decided they wanted to know how, and it has a puzzle-like fun about it. So anyways, here I am looking at one of the most beautiful things that really has ever happened to me. My own daughters! Gathered around an heirloom! Helping me! An intergenerational sewing circle making something for an as-yet unborn next generation! All with an incredible view of the ocean and sunshine streaming in the windows. It's probably something that I would have dreamed up in a really daydreamy time.

It was glorious. But it was also very real. And this sort of thing is very important to notice, especially so in an age of social media, where I could have taken a photo of that and posted it and everyone would have gotten the same idyllic moment feelings. Glorious things that happen in the real world happen . . . in the real world.

The finish on the rental house table had gotten sticky. There are few things I despise in life as much as the feeling of a sticky table on your forearms when you are trying to do something. There were also sand and crumbs on the floor, and as it turns out, the way that I like to organize my work is not the same way that all of my daughters intuitively do so. Bags of popcorn were making an appearance on the table, and crushed cans. The sun was shining, but it was just a little bit stuffy in the room. People were taking my scissors and putting them on the other end of the table, and once my daughters were really into it, I didn't fit into the space as well.

The moment was beautiful, but it was also REAL. Those minor annoyances did not make the moment less special or powerful or glorious. But they did give me an invitation to be a petty monster. They invited me to miss one of the most beautiful things that has ever happened to me because of an annoying sensation on my forearms.

This may be a silly example, but it is a very real problem that women everywhere must learn how to cope with. Life is real. The beautiful things never happen in a vacuum where there are no ugly or difficult things at the same time. The world is fallen, and any pursuit of a good and godly and glorious thing will be peppered with opportunities to not enjoy it, to be discouraged, to get distracted with a sad and selfish attitude that only wants to find the popcorn crumbs and the sticky table and the lost scissors and the stuffy air. Beautiful, precious, fuzzy-headed newborns also spit up and wake up in the night. Your body, having done its most epic and glorious work ever, will hurt and sag and be a little confused. So do not go into projects like the ones on the list I gave you with the expectation that roasting a chicken will be a dream and there will not be any struggle to it.

So this week I guess I want you all to do two things. First, go through that list together and mark all the things that you can already confidently do. Then pick something that you will work on this week. Maybe you can teach some of these skills to each other, or maybe one of you has a mom who would be happy to teach something to a whole group of you at once.

The second thing I want you to do is think about some moment in your life that was truly beautiful in its essence, but didn't feel beautiful because of the lifeyness of it all. Maybe your mother wanted to teach you something and you were just noticing everything that provokes you. Then ask yourself what it would take for you to appreciate the good and the true and the beautiful about these kinds of moments without giving into the kinds of temptations that abound in the middle of them. Remember how much the Enemy would like to keep you from doing these things that are truly so powerful. Be a lot harder to distract and neutralize.

I may as well end this overblown letter with one of my favorite quotes from I know not who: "Be the kind of woman that when her feet hit the floor in the morning the Devil says 'Oh crap! She's up!'" That is a woman who isn't easily deterred—the kind of woman we should all want to be.

Blessings on you all and all of your projects!
Aunt Lizzie

LETTER 16

# Body Image

Dear girls,

I am so glad to hear that you are having fun digging into so many things to learn. I love the question about the best cookbooks. The reality is that I have a great many of them and have used different ones for different things through the years. I find Ina Garten to be a very reliable source. Her food is very accessible and very delicious—if you think a recipe sounds good, it will be good. I also like *The New Best Recipe* from America's Test Kitchen. There is an awful lot in there, and it is an educational read. Every recipe starts with an introduction about all the ways they tested it and why they settled on certain methods and not others.

But honestly I think it is more fun to read widely in food-related things and choose the things that sound amazing to you to make. Our favorite recipes do not come from one place but rather from so many different places. You never know where you might find a treasure!

Now, about the dieting question. You have certainly put your finger on one of life's little troubles. But before we get to how to juggle your weight with being the person who makes the best cinnamon rolls, I want to back up a little and just talk about body image.

In your stage of life, you are all likely very self-aware about your bodies. This could be either a positive or negative self-consciousness. Maybe you are always tugging your sweatshirt down to cover up your belly, or maybe you are always tucking your shirt in a little tighter to show off your tiny waist. But instead of indulging in self-conscious shame or self-conscious pride, now is the time to establish a really normal, steady, and balanced relationship with your body.

Your body, Lord willing, is only just getting started on all the work that it will be used for. So you need to be a steward of your body more than a preserver of it. Having a baby will cost your body something. Having a bunch of babies will cost your body much. But it is a wonderful investment.

We live in an era where that particular expense is commonly seen as horrific and too much to ask of anyone. But here is the thing. Even if you give yourself to the preservation of your body and decide to never ever spend it on anything that will give you stretch marks and saggy boobs or extra weight—well, guess what? You will still grow old and get saggy. You just won't have anything to show for it.

Your youth is already spending itself with every passing day. Being a good steward of your body means making wise investments with it, and understanding and expecting difficulty in the life your body is going to live.

First and foremost, healthy body image means that you have a healthy relationship with God. God gave your body to you, and He should be praised for the generosity of that gift. There was no reason that you deserved a nose or hands or hair at all. Your body, no matter how you feel about how it looks, is a wild and undeserved blessing. Thank the Lord for it, and offer it back to the Lord. You should be able to look at yourself in the mirror and praise God. That is a healthy body image. Instead of looking at yourself and pretending you are the god of the system and saying "My body does not please me," look at yourself in the mirror and pray "Thank you Lord for this body, and may it please You as I use it for Your glory."

Now if you look in the mirror and really like what you see, you still need to thank the Lord for your body, remembering that you had nothing to do with it. Your body is not your doing, it is not permanently yours, and it is to be used wisely and well in glorifying God and enjoying Him forever. Even if you have no reason to dislike your body at this moment, there will almost certainly come a time in your life where you will need to process what is happening to your body in light of this relationship to your Creator. All around us, the world is trying to please themselves with their bodies, plumping up their lips with shots, worrying over every wrinkle and crease, getting implants or nose jobs and trying to ice or vacuum out fat. Yet what evades them is the ultimate secret to aging gracefully—which is aging *in grace*. Faithfully tend your relationship to your Creator, and use your body gladly. This will set up a wonderful framework for caring for your body throughout your life.

When you are right with God on that fundamental level, you will find that it is much easier and more intuitive to deal with the things you need to do for your body. Stewardship of your body may mean you really do need to lose twenty pounds. Acknowledging this does not need to feel like an emotional armageddon. It may just be facts. All of the emotions in all of the land will not make the work you need to do easier. In fact, the emotions are far more likely to cause extra trouble. Many a young girl takes off on a horrible diet that is driven by fear, guilt, or shame and just ends up treating herself to some long-term metabolic problems or bad habits or secret sins. Whatever you are doing to care for your body, or whatever you need to do, do it like a sensible woman. Make sure that the methods you decide to use are things you could talk about out loud to sensible people without shocking them.

Many a young girl cultivates some kind of a disordered eating habit without ever really meaning to. Some studies say that as many as three in four young women have an eating disorder.

These disorders are usually cultivated as a secret response to personal fear. Christian women ought not to be driven by negative emotions into foolish behaviors and patterns.

Imagine that for some reason (even you do not know why) you ate too much. You really overindulged and you feel gross and you can't believe that you lost control like that . . . and what kind of a person even *does* that? In this situation, you should simply ask the Lord to forgive you for your loss of self-control, and ask Him to teach you moderation and wisdom in and through this discomfort.

You must not try to undo your loss of self-control by grasping after a different kind of control that you should not have. Vomiting up a sinful episode only adds to the sin. The only god who could be pleased with an offering of vomited donuts is a god you do not want to serve—one with a toilet for an altar, one whose worship can only be accomplished in secret. You are a free woman, and you know the God who made you free—so you must not believe the lies that simply slipping into this or that bad habit will make you feel better or somehow vindicate your behavior. RUN away from such temptation.

Concentrate on a relationship of gratitude and thanksgiving with your Creator God. Anchor your thinking in reality. Right at the center of our faith is a table that was laid for us by our Creator—partake of that fellowship rightly, and you will be able to rightly partake of other food at other tables. Do not lie to yourself, and do not be easy to lie to. Are you vulnerable to almost anything that is suggested to you by a celebrity or by someone who does not look like they have the problems you have? Orthorexia, for example, is an obsession with eating healthy food only—and while it may look good on the internet, it is not at all good for you. We can all be very gullible. The more you acknowledge this reality, the better your life will be.

> For of this sort are those who creep into households and make captives of gullible women loaded down with sins, led away by various lusts. (2 Tim. 3:6)

The thing that I want to draw your attention to in this passage is the last part. Do not set yourself up to be taken captive by all kinds of hateful worldviews and ideologies by harboring little sins and indulging little lusts. Those are the handles which are used to take you captive. Focus on clear and simple confession of sin, and you will not be nearly as gullible.

Obviously this passage is not about eating disorders specifically, but it certainly applies. And it applies just as easily to a porn problem as it does to anorexia. It applies to any sin or foolishness in your thought life, or anything that you would really rather never speak to anyone about.

Note that these bad actors *creep* into households. The need for secrecy is a big red flag. If it really matters to you that you have total secrecy—if no one who loves you would understand what you're doing—you are almost certainly enslaved to something that you need help to deal with. If you think you really need to lose weight, and you don't tell anybody because you know that all of your friends and your parents and anyone on the street would tell you that you absolutely do not need to, that is a sure sign that you have been taken captive by something ugly.

If this describes you at all—if you have a secret life of the mind that makes dieting rules for you, makes you do penance by vomiting, makes you pretend to eat or pretend to not eat, leads you to sneak off to watch something you should not be watching—that is a big sign that you need outside help. There are some kinds of thoughts that die immediately upon being brought into the open air. Hasten them there. Get real accountability. You should probably start with your mom.

Your secret sin is no secret. Not only does your Heavenly Father know about it; so do others. If you have watched a little porn, and you feel like this is between just you and yourself, you need to think again. It is between you and the *world wide web*. It is between you and the people who will remember what you've seen and market things to you accordingly. The predators who are after your soul will avail themselves of every possible hold over you. The fact that you are currently hiding that handle on your heart from your parents does not make it invisible to the Enemy who is holding fast to it. Porn is a theatrical production put on by slaves—and whoever comes into that theater is a sitting duck, asking to be enslaved as well.

So after all of that, we can finally come back around to the simple question we started with: How can we make pans of cinnamon rolls without looking like a pan of cinnamon rolls ourselves?

First of all, we should not be afraid of the good gifts that the Lord has given us. That includes butter and sugar and flour and the ability to put those things together into something greater than the individual parts. It also includes the ability to enjoy things like cinnamon rolls reasonably and with gratitude. The Lord has given us His Spirit, who can help us to learn this all-important self-control.

If you are going to be a wife and mother, you are going to be in a position where it is your job to bless people with food (which you yourself should not overindulge in). This is not a problem, but you will need to develop strong self-control. Since we already need this skill and ability in every other area of our lives, we should welcome more training opportunities.

If you think that learning to bake delicious things will wind up making you fat, then you probably need to work on self-control anyways. As a mother of sons I have grown used to making all manner of things that I don't even taste. It turns out that the nutritional needs of growing young men are not the same as a forty-three-year-old woman! Who would have thought?

I realize that we have just covered a lot of major personal topics in a big breeze-by. Well, such is life! Love to you all, and if this conversation prompted you to think of a secret sin that has a stranglehold on you, let me encourage you to take that seriously and get help outside of your own secret resolutions. There is hope. There is help. You can be forgiven and you can be free. Don't shy away because you know that the remedy for the sin will hurt. Unconfessed sin is infinitely more painful than any confession will ever be. It's far better to clean out a small wound than to have to remove a limb.

I should mention here that if you have a secret sin problem that is haunting you, it is very, very hard to just stop. While you certainly do need to stop, you will be far more successful if you fight the sin with positive action. Take for example a sinful thought. Now imagine yourself focusing entirely on not thinking it. This sort of thing really reveals our human frailty. Thinking to yourself "Don't worry don't worry don't worry" is in itself worrying. My mom has always described the right way to fight sin as "changing the radio station." It's not enough to stop doing the wrong thing; you need to actively set your mind on things above (Col. 3:2).

This is something that you can help each other do without rummaging in the basement of everyone's hearts and sharing all of your worst troubles with each other. You can provide strong accountability in the light without digging into the darkness. Be open and free about your Bible reading, about the positive good things that you should be filling both your mind and your time with. You can be a tremendous help to one another in fighting sin, not so much by talking about your temptations all of the time, but rather by helping each other set your minds on things above. Look up. Look to Christ. Encourage one another to press on by pressing on together.

Also, and I'm not even kidding, learn to bake cinnamon rolls. Here is our classic family recipe. Although I have certainly made and enjoyed other cinnamon rolls, the way we like them is light and fluffy and soft, with a light icing rather than a cream cheese frosting. These are the cinnamon rolls of my childhood, and they really do behave pretty well. This will give you a great starting point to work with!

Much love,
Aunt Lizzie

# Cinnamon Triumph Rolls

YIELD: 12 (OR 24 SMALL ROLLS)

## INGREDIENTS

- 3 c. Warm Water
- 2/3 c. Sugar
- 2 tsp. Salt
- 2 tbsp. Yeast
- 2 Eggs, beaten
- 2/3 c. Shortening
- 1 tsp. Vanilla
- 8–9 c. All-Purpose Flour

## FOR THE FILLING

- 1/2 c. Butter, softened
- 1 c. Sugar
- 4 tsp. Cinnamon

## FOR THE GLAZE

- 2 c. Powdered Sugar
- Milk or cream—add to desired consistency

## DIRECTIONS

1. Mix together the water, sugar, and salt. Add the yeast and stir until dissolved. Add the eggs, shortening, and vanilla. Add enough flour while mixing to make a soft dough that is not too sticky to handle.
2. Dump the dough out on a lightly floured surface and knead until smooth, adding flour if you need it to keep the dough from clinging to your hands. When you have a soft and smooth dough, put a little oil in a large plastic bowl and put your dough in it. Flip the dough over so that there is oil on top, cover with a tea towel, and let it rise until doubled (an hour or so).
3. Roll or pat the dough out on a lightly floured surface to make a large rectangle—18"x24". Spread the whole surface with the softened butter, then sprinkle the sugar and cinnamon all over the dough. Roll the dough up, starting on the long end closest to you and keeping the roll tight. Pinch the edge to seal it into a big log.

4. At this point you can stretch the log out to 48" to make 24 smaller rolls or keep it at 24" for 12 large ones.
5. Preheat the oven to 375 degrees.
6. Cut the roll with a bread knife every two inches or so and place the cinnamon rolls evenly on a half-sized baking sheet, about an inch apart. Pat them gently to even them out. Cover and let rise for 30 minutes. If you need more time, you can put them straight into the fridge after cutting for a longer second rise.
7. Bake for 30–35 minutes, or until the rolls in the center of the sheet are just getting a little bit golden. I usually pull a couple apart very gently in the middle to check that they are bready all the way through and not doughy at all.
8. Stir the powdered sugar and milk/cream together to create a powdered sugar glaze. Start with a little—the more milk/cream, the thinner the glaze. While the rolls are still warm, drizzle the glaze over the top.

   *Note: A delicious variation is to spread a jar of marmalade as the filling and make a glaze of orange juice and powdered sugar.*

# LETTER 17
# Pornography

Dear Maddie,

I want to reassure you right away that I am glad you wrote me! I do not mind at all that you reached out separately from our big group discussion! I am sorry to hear that you have been struggling so much, but I am SO THANKFUL that the Holy Spirit is not letting you press on without confronting it. What a blessing that is, even though it may not feel like it. Right now, you are probably just feeling sad and hopeless and confused—but God is offering you joy, and hope, and clarity. The Holy Spirit seems to have His hand on you, and while you are experiencing that primarily as guilt right now, it is actually the ultimate kindness. You are a loved daughter, and your Heavenly Father is not leaving you in your sin but rather calling you right out of it. So do not despair. There is lots of good news for you ahead.

From all of the things that you mentioned, it seems to me like your tangle of sin all comes back to one central problem: the habit of consuming is consuming you. Here's what I mean.

Probably without thinking, you have parked yourself with your phone and told the world to bring you anything it wants you to sample. It sounds like your life on the internet started with feeling left out. This may seem like an innocent beginning. But looking at what everyone else is doing in order to keep track of every detail and every sign of how you are not being valued or included is just another form of self-pity. Self-pity is destructive. Envy is a destroyer. All of this started with you feeling left out, but now it's ending with you being included in things you never meant to be a part of.

This insecurity (thinking no one wants you) led to you looking enviously at women who are wanted, which naturally bloomed into a habit of looking at porn. This fueled your increasing feelings of self-loathing and insecurity about your body, which is at least a factor in the binge-eating and dieting. The guilt over it all has slowly become the background noise of your life so that everything feels tainted by it. I don't know if you have stepped back far enough from your feelings on this to observe how predictable this cause and effect has been.

The more you are unhappy about your weight, the more you are inclined to feel slighted and be consumed with your own feelings. The more you let those feelings lead you around, the more your feelings get used to being in charge of you, and the more it seems that you are standing around waiting for your feelings to tell you what is next. Shall we go eat ice cream in secret and indulge in hating ourselves, or should we go look at porn again and indulge in hating ourselves? Whichever way you end up going, the motive is the same: an urgency to consume something to make yourself feel something. It always ends in self-loathing and shame.

There is no *easy* way out of this. Disrupting the bad patterns and habits you have made will take a lot of hard work. I am sure that after you wrote me you had second thoughts and wished you hadn't pulled the trigger on the whole issue like that. But I am so glad that you did!

Here are a few things that we know about God. He loves you. He knows exactly what you have been doing, and He is gracious and willing to forgive you. He has made forgiveness for you possible in the work of His Son on the cross. He delights to set prisoners free. He delights to give wisdom. He delights to take our sins and put them as far away from us as the east is from the west. He is a gracious and loving Father. This is why looking at your sin and acknowledging it freely is a gift—you don't have to keep it!

So the way out is not easy, but it really is simple. Here's what you need to do. First, confess your sins to God. Start with the big obvious ones. Get those right with God by acknowledging them and asking for His forgiveness. Now, because you are at home and your parents are paying for your phone and for the internet and for your food, you also need to make things right with them. Tell them that you have repented of your sin to God, but that you are also repenting of it to them. You need their forgiveness, and you also need the accountability that they did not realize you needed. So get things right with them and ask them for practical help in upsetting the patterns you have established.

If your relationship with your parents is uncomfortable and uneasy such that you cannot imagine talking to them about this and anticipate it making more trouble than it could ever solve, then you should make an appointment with your pastor or his wife and start there instead. I did not get this feeling from your first letter, but I want to be clear about this anyways. The important thing here is that you get help from someone who knows you in real life and is a responsible Christian. If the situation with your parents is a loaded or complicated one, you may need pastoral support in negotiating that.

I want to hear back from you on how this goes! I'll be praying that the Lord abundantly blesses your efforts to walk faithfully and deal with these besetting sins. When you no longer have a big tangle of current and unconfessed sin hanging over your head, I want to talk more with you about what I believe are the root causes of all this. I think that will help you root things out before they become so overwhelming.

The LORD bless you and keep you;
The LORD make His face shine upon you,
And be gracious to you;
The LORD lift up His countenance upon you,
And give you peace. (Num. 6:24–26)

With love and prayers,
Aunt Lizzie

# LETTER 18
# Boys

Dear girls,

I am glad to hear you are doing so well! I am proud of the way you are all just rolling your sleeves up and jumping in. I also love to hear that you have made a superabundance of cinnamon rolls—what a fun idea to take them for the after-church fellowship time. I hope everybody liked them! They do freeze well, in case you ever need to know that.

What I want to talk about today is pretty much in the "street smart" and "know thyself" categories. This is the kind of advice I would give and have given my daughters—the random things that are part of being a woman who sees her behavior honestly and wants to use her body wisely and not foolishly.

First off, you are not as physically strong as you may think that you are. For a variety of reasons, the world spends a lot of time pretending that women and men have basically the same abilities. But a beautiful woman in high heels and a leather jacket could not actually throw a much bigger man on the ground and get his hands into handcuffs while she is on the phone with a friend. This is simply not the case, although it has happened many times on the television. Even if you are a very fit, very strong woman, a very middling man is probably quite a bit more than you can handle.

Now this information ought to factor into the way you behave. You ought not to be living in fear, but you also ought to stay away from situations that you could not easily get out of (both physically and emotionally). Do not get a ride to a party with someone who may or may not want to leave when you may want to leave. I have known many girls who ended up violating their own standards and conscience because they did not have an exit plan. You need to be able to get yourself out of a situation that turns out to be unwise, and you do not want to be dependent on the discretion of a dumb friend. Think ahead about what could go wrong, and ask yourself how you would deal with it if it did. Be prepared. What if the movie turns out to be inappropriate? What if people are behaving foolishly? What if there is a guy at this party you don't know who is making you uncomfortable? Get yourself out of the situation and do it quickly.

Young women need practice saying no and sticking to it. It is a good idea to give it a try in the mirror. Say something like "No thank you, I am not interested," and try to do it without hastening to look away or feeling panicky (or at the very least without *looking* panicky).

It matters that you take responsibility for the situations you find yourself in, whether the stakes are big or small. You can do this graciously and in a kind and wise manner. However, you have to accustom yourself to taking ownership of your own body and situation, and you have to be able to make a decision, make that decision clear to others as needed, and then stick to your decision, no matter the resistance.

Now I say all of this without accusing any particular boy of any particular motive. But when you get into a situation where a young man (or an older one, or occasionally another woman!) imposes on you in some way, you need to be able to actively resist the change which their unexpected behavior is making to your relationship.

There is almost always a dynamic between young men and women that is pure power struggle. What you want to avoid is any kind of submissive posture to a man that you owe no submission to. If a random guy you know comes up and leans on you, it is important that you not freeze up and let him do it just because it feels awkward to say something. In the long run, it is far more awkward to blithely accept him treating you like his beast of burden.

These sorts of awkward situations are just facts of life, and every woman needs to be prepared to deal graciously and well with them. If you do not ever resist, you are doing two things wrong: you are training other people to impose on you *against your judgment*, and you are training yourself to be a doormat. Just because these things begin happening in trivial matters does not mean that they are trivial relationship dynamics.

One little pushback is often all it takes to establish clarity between you. It will feel awkward because it is awkward. Recognize that the feeling of discomfort *is the tool* that is being used against you to impose on you. The way to resist it is by not being afraid of the awkward discomfort. I have a friend who in her youth walked into a public rest stop at night. In the otherwise empty women's bathroom was a huge man, with his foot on the counter, pulling up his fishnet tights. She panicked. It feels so awkward to act like something is wrong—wrong with him being here, wrong with what he is doing, wrong with her being the person to encounter it. In a social-awkwardness-induced panic, she hustled into a stall acting like nothing was wrong. Praise the Lord that this man left while she was in there and nothing else happened with him. But it is a great example of how a sweet Christian girl would take all of the awkwardness of a sinful man on herself and try to pretend that everything is *fine*.

To be clear, by "imposing on you," I'm not talking about a guy asking if you could please pass the salt. There is no need to kick up a fuss about something like that. But if a guy asks you to rub sunscreen on his back, do not just think "Oh I guess we do this now." You've got to get good at the awkward no. Imagine a guy helps himself to your coffee. Don't just act like "Well, I guess we share drinks now." Instead, simply refuse to take it back from him. Let him sit in the awkwardness while you continue on, undramatic and unaffected. If a guy sits down too close to you on a couch, get up and let him have the seat to himself, however silly it feels. Say something like "Forgive me, I seem to have been in your way." If a guy uses your chapstick without permission, let him keep it. Just laughingly say "I certainly don't want it now!"

If you are walking down the street and accidentally make eye contact with a guy walking toward you, control your automatic urge to look down. This is one of those little things that communicates a lot. Instead, look directly to the side of his eyes as though there is something much more interesting just behind him. Keep your head up. Or if a guy is inexplicably rude to you, do not look down. Do not be pushed into embarrassed and submissive behavior by shock tactics. Try instead a simple question like "Why are you being so rude? Do you think it makes you attractive?"

These are all examples of situations where a young man might assert himself in order to see how you'll respond. Are you willing to let him impose on you? I hope not. Even if he is a wonderful guy who you believe may be a candidate for a future husband, you need to be harder to get than that. Do not fall into a submissive posture toward a man who has no lawful and respectable authority over you. Be the awkward that you know I want to see in the world. Have a standard and stick to it, even if he has stormy eyes and is gazing at you with them.

This kind of behavior is profoundly *ladylike.* This is not an excuse for you to become rudey-tudey. If a young man you are not enchanted with opens the door for you, it is nonetheless your job to politely say thank you and go through it. Things like offering you a chair and letting you go first in line are not impositions, just manners. So don't get all combative all the time.

We have talked about the ways to not let a boy impose on you, but I also want you to be careful to not impose on them. Do not use your body to cause social confusion for him—it is not ladylike or polite. Don't brush up against him, or lean over in front of him. Don't stand a little too close so you have to look up into his face to talk to him through your eyelashes in a quiet voice. Have enough cynicism about your own motives that you recognize that you are trying to stumble him or cloud his judgment. Even if you are good future wife material (aside from this present bad behavior), this is no way a godly young man should want to be caught.

He *ought* to avoid you when he notices that this is what you are doing. He ought to recognize that no human woman needs to sit on the floor like the mud flap girl making sure the whole room gets a view of her silhouette, having prepared for this important opportunity by wearing a too-tight T-shirt and a push-up bra. He ought to resist that kind of behavior from you in the same way you ought to resist a man randomly trying to dominate you.

Do not despise the standards that any godly young man ought to have simply because your heart wants to be the object of his desire. Many a young couple who get into sin together (even when they go on to get married and live "happily ever after") have accidentally built a relationship on this kind of mutual disrespect. Women do not respect men who are easily led astray, even when they have used themselves as the bait.

So this week I want you to practice saying no, in the mirror and/or with each other. Do it in a ladylike manner, but try to do it in a way that is not budgeable and leaves no room for debate. I also want you to think about how to comport yourself like a wise woman and not a wily one. Wisdom values and loves boundaries. It respects them and upholds them. So think of any ways that you have messed around with barriers and root that out—in your heart first, but then possibly in your closet and your body language and your makeup drawer. Look for wisdom, pursue wisdom—even in these little places.

With love,
Aunt Lizzie

P.S. Even if you have some funny interactions with guys, be careful to not be gossipy or belittle them to one another. Girls can be very foolishly free with their opinions of the young men: "I could never in a million years be interested in *him* . . ." Just keep in mind that you could always be mouthing off about how unattractive you find a man to the girl who will marry him. It's best to be ladylike and keep such thoughts close. You do not need to submit a public review of every young man of your acquaintance, and it is beyond foolish to get in that habit. Be generally respectful of others, which is not the same thing as being a pushover.

# LETTER 19

# Envy

Dear Maddie,

I am so thankful to hear that your talk with your parents went better than you expected. It is not at all surprising to me that it was embarrassing, but what a gift that it was encouraging and relieving as well.

What you described is actually very common! Many parents who were saved later in life assume that some of their old temptations and sins bogged them down only because they were not yet believers. Because of that, they can sometimes fail to be on the lookout on behalf of their own children, assuming that growing up in a Christian home automatically inoculates them from some kinds of sin. It's great that you have their accountability now, and I am hopeful that this will help in a lot of little ways.

I mentioned the last time we talked that I wanted to come back at some point and revisit what I think is ground zero for a lot of this.

Given how you described the tangle that you were in, I think it is safe to say that both the disordered eating and the porn trouble got traction in your life because you felt out of control and wanted to feel in control. The stress in one area of your life led to you trying to exert control over yourself in other areas. You indulged wildly in eating things because you wanted a rush of good feeling that you could be in control of. Watching porn was just another way of doing the same thing. As we both know, neither of these things helped you in any way. Immediately afterward, you were faced with self-loathing, shame, etc. But the question I want you to think and pray about is this: What kind of internal narrative were you indulging in that got your stress and loneliness and anxiety to such a level in the first place?

Your first letter made it clear that this whole downward spiral started with you feeling left out and lonely. But it also sounds like you think those lonely feelings were a result of other people's failings. If the girls around you had been more kind and inclusive, you might never have spiraled in the first place. As another step toward dealing with your own sin all the way down, I'd like you to look back at that assumption with new eyes.

I'm guessing social media is playing a role here. The fact that you are aware of everyone else's social engagements tells me that you have a lot of spies out there in the world, reporting back to you on everything that you want to feel bad about. You weren't invited to that concert, other people did their nails together without you, etc.

I don't mean to be harsh here—because I am well-aware that teenagers can be real turkeys in their efforts to impress each other with their fun times. Even if it isn't malicious, sharing every moment of your life in a filtered picture as though you are having a great time all the time is not healthy. But it is even less healthy for *you* to have your face pressed up against this imaginary window, always looking at what you think you are being left out of. Maybe the people on the other side of that window could be more kind to you, more thoughtful—but it is entirely your responsibility to not fall into sin about it. Yes, I said *sin*. It is a sin to troll around the internet looking for things to hurt your feelings. It is a sin to fall into social voyeurism—touring around imagining what everyone else is enjoying that you wish you had. This is just envy.

When I was in high school we had track shirts that said "Don't look back—you're not running that way." I have since used that phrase as an example with my children. If you are running your fastest, you really can't afford to be looking off to the side all the time. You will, undoubtedly, run straight into a great big envy tree and knock yourself out of the race. Envy is never okay, and should always be confessed as a sin. So if there are specific people that you know you have been consistently envying, by all means confess that. Thank the Lord for them, for the good gifts that He has given them, and then mentally change the channel. Stop thinking about it.

I would also strongly encourage you to get off of every social platform that you have been using to fill your mental life. Get your parents to change your passwords. When you do this, it probably won't be long before you start craving a good look-about so you can have a self-pity party. As soon as you notice that happening, confess it. Recognize that this is the first wave of the cycle that has been putting you in such a despairing tangle.

I want you to think about the binge-eating and the porn use as a line that you cross halfway down a waterslide. You know those sins are destructive. But what you need to get good at is recognizing where you're headed up at the top of the slide. Up there, the sin looks fairly innocent. But now that you have seen what envy can do to you, you need to acknowledge that this whole thing is not a good idea. The sin started with getting on the slide in the first place, and did not spontaneously become a problem halfway down.

I am encouraging you to cut things out of your life. But it's just as important to fill your time up with productive things. Don't just sit around staring at your phone and thinking about how you could look at it. Find real things in the real world to work on. You're in the middle of rooting out some ginormous thistles, and a very effective form of weed management is to plant and maintain and nourish things that are *not weeds*.

One other thing I want to say before I go, and that is GOOD JOB! I am so thankful for this wonderful growth in your life. You are dealing with a sinful pattern like a woman of God. You are confessing sin and pursuing righteousness. Don't ever be discouraged by where you *are* when where you are *heading* is in the absolute right direction—to Christ, always to Christ, and in the power of the Holy Spirit.

May the Lord bless you and keep you in His abundant kindness!

With love,
Aunt Lizzie

# LETTER 20
# Husbands

Dear girls,

I enjoyed all the thoughts you had about learning to say no. I especially love that it felt so foreign and uncomfortable to you all. That is certainly a sign that this is really important for you to think about.

As with many things in the process of maturing, saying no is something of an artistic endeavor. You need to know when you should be immovable and when you need instead to be flexible, glad to help, not resentful of the fact that someone presumed you would be willing to contribute or share. These sorts of things are always in tension. You need to have a firm (and always growing) understanding of the principles that you intend to live by, and then you need to develop the skill of making decisions on the fly about situations that you could not have anticipated in advance. Work carefully and proceed prayerfully and learn from the stupid mistakes you make when you intend to be wise! As tough situations come up, talk to your parents about them. Ask them if what you did was the right thing, and if there was anything you could have done differently.

Especially in the realm of your relationships with guys, I want you to be really aware of the fact that impositions are not neutral. There is usually something else going on under the surface. This is one of those places where it is common for Christian girls to have the idea that "niceness equals godliness." But niceness can lead you into going along with things that you ought not to. You do need to be kind and sweet and submissive—but in the right places. In other places you need to be absolutely impossible to deal with. Like I said, it's a balancing act!

The biggest trouble I ever got into in high school was over the dumbest bit of cowardice. I had gotten permission to go with some other teens on a walk, and I didn't expect to get picked up in a car. Once in the car, I was surprised to hear we were going hiking instead and were off on a drive to the location. The plans had changed and no one had consulted me.

Because I did not want to inconvenience or impose on other people, or be the awkward girl who was not allowed to go anymore, I disobeyed my parents and tried to make truth-bending excuses for myself. Since this was before the time of cell phones, I could not call my parents to explain my dilemma—and it really was a dilemma! On the one hand, it is generally a good idea to not inconvenience other people. You could make a pretty Christian-sounding argument for my decision. Lay your life down for others! Think of others as more important than yourself! But the reality is that I should have prioritized obeying my parents and being back when I said I would be back over and above the awkwardness that it would have caused. I didn't want to say "Actually never mind, I need you to take me home." I learned the importance of taking ownership of my own obedience during this worst hike I ever went on. It was no fun from beginning to guilty end, and it would have been vastly better to just be awkward and say "No, actually I can't come."

Now I know that you are all mostly interested in when it will be a good idea for you to say yes to a guy—not just no no no all the day long. Up to now, I have been talking to you about not taking on a submissive posture toward the guys in general. But the fact remains that, as Christian women, you are going to need to take on a submissive role when the Lord brings a good man into your life. And at that time, yes. You should say yes.

Still, even when this good man comes along, you do not *begin* by submitting to him. You wait to submit until you are both in a covenanted relationship and he has made vows before God and witnesses to love, honor, and protect you. You don't ever want to get into that kind of relationship until you have full confidence in the faithfulness of that man. When you first meet him, you should actually be noticing that you *respect* him. This is not the same thing as finding him hard to resist.

There is a world of difference between a man who knows how to *push you* into things and a man who knows how to *lead you*. I've been warning you to not be pushable—but being leadable is another matter altogether. I hope you can see how a cute boy with a sparkle in his eye and an attractive, mischief-making demeanor could push you into things that you didn't mean to do and know that you should not be doing. This is a brutal and very sad setup for a marriage. A man who pushed you to get what he wanted is often not respectable. Likeability and respectability are not the same thing.

This is why it is downright foolish for girls to "crush" on guys, or talk about hypothetical crushes (like celebrity crushes). You shouldn't practice cultivating an interest in attractive men who don't have principles. You shouldn't practice falling for a guy and showing no discretion. Why would you want to be the kind of woman who is bowled over by dimples or a cowboy hat or a five-o'clock shadow? We should care more about the things that are actually important, and not so much about the things that can be pulled off by anyone who happened to be born handsome.

To respect a man means that you find him trustworthy. You know that he is pursuing God, that he is not a danger to you, and that if you were to follow him, he would lead you in paths of righteousness. If there is such a guy, by all means respect him.

But respecting him as a godly man is not done by looking up at him while fluttering your eyelashes or dreaming of how you would look on his arm. Preparing for marriage is not the same thing as curating Pinterest boards of cute wedding venues. Don't spend time imagining a "hot man" placeholder in your dreams of matrimony, which are really just dreams of photo shoots and other details that do not and will not matter.

You should respect your father, your pastor, your elders, your boss, and many other people. What is unique about the man you marry is that you take vows to submit to him. Paul calls wives to respect their husbands (Eph. 5:33) and submit to their husbands (Eph. 5:22). These are not optional ideas. Once you are married, these are relational duties that you will need to uphold. It will not be a question of "Can I respect this man?" but rather "How can I respect this man?" It behooves every young woman to look honestly at that moral obligation and recognize that you don't want to get yourself into a relationship with someone who is not a wise choice. Your husband will hold a very important office in your life.

It is also important to understand that respect, like love, does not always occur naturally. Sometimes you need to choose to respect someone because God told you to, not because their behavior is just inspiring it in you.

I hope that you have all been taught already that men thrive on respect in the same way that women thrive on love. Women, when they are feeling unloved, often act surpassingly unloveable. Men, when they are feeling disrespected, often act surpassingly unrespectable. Obviously both genders need both love and respect—but Scripture emphasizes men's need for respect and women's need for love in a way that makes it clear the difference matters.

So the duty of a husband is to keep on giving love as Christ loved, even in those moments where lovability is at a low point. And the duty of a wife is to keep on giving respect, straight through those moments that are not the most respect-inspiring. When women refuse to respect where they have a duty to be respectful, they are *depriving themselves* of something that is essential for them to thrive. There is something in the makeup of a woman that goes quickly rank and sour when she ceases to give respect where she should. This is where the world gets its bitter, accusing, nitpicky, thin-souled women. This is the fast track to uglytown.

There is something about rendering respect where you owe it (in spite of your husband's failings or shortcomings) that is downright *nutritious* and beautifying for women. It is not just good for him to have your respect—it is good for you to render it. Obeying God brings out the best in us, always. Disobeying God does exactly the opposite. You can see how the same is true for men. The worst of men comes out when they despise those who are entitled to their love and protection. Their failure doesn't only harm the women and children who should be receiving their love—it destroys their own souls as well. What you don't want to do is sign yourself up for a very, very hard lot in life, with an unrespectable but once-handsome man.

So for now—don't be pushed into things. Respect the men who are already in positions of authority in your life.

Always remember you must only submit to human authorities where it is consistent with submitting to God. Pray for your future husband, that he would be faithfully growing in the Lord—and then do all that you can to be the kind of woman that a man like that ought to want to marry. Spend your time saying yes, in total submission, to the Word of God. That will require a lot of other no's in your life, but it is wonderful preparation for the time when you will meet a man to say yes to. Beyond that, it will make that "yes" something that was worth winning!

Until next week,
Aunt Lizzie

LETTER 21

# Leadership

Dear Lottie,

This has been a great time, and I am glad that you have enjoyed it—I have too!

I think it is perfectly natural that what has developed is a sort of core group of friends who are "all in," for want of a better term. This is a gift, and not something you should feel at all guilty about. It is good to have friends who are doing the same things as you and who are interested in pursuing the next level of maturity together. It is healthy to periodically invite new people to join you in things—that'll keep you from becoming a clique in an unkind way. But a solid group of good friends is not a thing to feel guilty about. Thank the Lord for it and press on.

Leadership is by definition a little bit lonely. This is true when you're leading many people, and it is true when you're leading a few toddlers at home. It seems clear to me that the Lord has put you in a natural position of leadership among your peers, and the things that are chafing you are very normal for anyone in that position. Why can't the other girls have a vision and push toward worthwhile goals without you leading the charge? Well, it's because God put you there! The body of Christ functions this way all the time. Someone once jokingly told me that in the body I am the pituitary gland—I want to see everyone being busy! And it is actually true. I love nothing more than a rally toward a vision—I dislike nothing so much as a lack of vision and action. What a mess the church body would be if we were all like me. It is important to recognize the gifts God has given you and to carefully cultivate them in such a way that they are gifts to the whole body. Every virtue comes with a vice. My strengths in this regard are the same thing as my weaknesses, which is why walking by faith and trusting the Lord is such an important thing. We all have to be cultivating our natural abilities in the Lord, diligently weeding sinful things out, thinking of others as more important than ourselves, and confessing our sins and failings as we find them. We will find them all over the place.

There is always the possibility of discontentment when you realize how much work this will be. It can be a temptation to look longingly at the life of girls who do not need to steward what you need to steward. Don't give in to that! The Lord knows what He is doing when He sets each one of us in our places—in our families, in our churches, in our culture, in our time. In the same way that we need to cultivate a healthy body image before the Lord, we need to cultivate a healthy personality image. Don't wish the Lord made you less than He did, or differently than He did. Don't try to undo the gifts that He gave you or the position He called you to. Your entire life and situation is a gift from Him, and you should spend your energy thinking instead of how to glorify God in and with it.

Now when you find yourself in a leadership position and you do not like the way things are going, one of the most fundamental things to keep in mind is *pull, don't push.* Do not let the fact that you have a bigger vision give you a critical spirit or turn you into an affliction to your friends. Try not to poke and prod your friends into doing more or wanting more. Don't nip at their heels. No one wants that. Instead, think in terms of getting out ahead and making your vision attractive. Pulling is always more effective than pushing. Pulling is also harder—it requires you to have a vision and take off toward it. Do not go after things that would be worthless if you and you alone did them. You have to want to do the thing with or without the support of followers.

Good and godly leadership is done in the Spirit and by the Spirit. It requires faith. What is fatal here is feeling sorry for yourself—feeling tragic about the fact that you alone have the vision. Just do everything that you can to enflesh that vision. Be full of gratitude, offering your work to God, and I am confident that that will be attractive. If it isn't, learn what you can from the experience and move on without angst.

It has been so fun to get to know you more through these letters—you remind me so much of your mom, and that is one of the best compliments I could give!

Many blessings, and until next time!
Aunt Lizzie

LETTER 22

# Dangerous Women

Dear girls,

I wanted to spend this last letter trying to dig into what all of this means. What are all of these little topics contributing toward? I can think of no better way of summarizing it than to say that I wish for you to be truly *dangerous women*.

As I mentioned before, there is an optical illusion when you are young that you really have a lot of time. I can guarantee you that you really, really don't. These years of your life are an opportunity to become thoroughly equipped for the many good works that the Lord has prepared for you. It would be a shame to waste them messing around on social media. Or watching stupid shows. Or falling into petty squabbles. Or cultivating foolish crushes. Or developing eating disorders. You have plenty of time for good things, but you just don't have time to be dumb.

Think of any story or movie where there is a big goal that will be hard to attain. What does the hero do? Think of the famous training scene in *Rocky*—where he is up early and drinking raw eggs and running through the streets of Philly and using a side of beef as a punching bag. He is driven by the fact that something important is coming that will require much of him. Now imagine the same training montage, but Rocky is eating gummy bears and milk duds, or napping on the couch, or getting drive-through, or eating cupcakes while watching *Ultimate Beastmaster*.

Now it's true that Rocky was preparing for an acute moment where he would need lots of physical strength and endurance and discipline, and obviously he is a man and you are young ladies. But you are preparing for *more* than one fight with Apollo Creed, not less. You are preparing for a lifetime that will demand strength and courage and discipline—a lifetime that will require more skills than good boxing. You are not called to fight one big fight, but rather to *live* like what you are doing matters. Your whole life is a conflict of light with darkness. So live in the joy of the Lord and pursue His glory. This work begins daily in your own heart.

When I say "dangerous women," I mean *dangerous* in the sense that you pose an actual threat to the enemies of God. I mean *dangerous* in the sense that you will grow to be godly, faithful women who are mothers and grandmothers and great-grandmothers and unknown ancestors to hoards of godly and faithful men and women. It is my prayer that each of you are at the headwaters of absolute *armies* of God, armies that will eat together and worship together and grow and sing and celebrate and share the Gospel and stamp out unbelief and darkness wherever they find it. It is my prayer that your homes will be full of light and that your doors will be flung open, inviting a weary and broken world to meet the King. It is my hope that when a godly man finds you and makes you his, he will have done something overwhelmingly *wise*. That you will be his crown of glory, that you will make his life fruitful and abundant, that you will be a blessing and not a curse to him all of his days. It is my prayer that the children who grow up in your homes will always know grace and mercy and joy and life because they met it first through you. There is no strength like the joy of the Lord, and it is my prayer that your descendants will be truly *mighty* in joy.

Redeem the time, for you have been redeemed.

Much love,
Aunt Lizzie

# About the Author

Rachel Jankovic is a wife, homemaker, and mother. She has written several books, including *You Who?* and *Loving the Little Years*—she's also one half of the What Have You podcast. She's married to Luke, and they have eight children who keep her doing whatever is next as fast as possible.